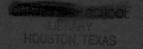

# THE NEW NUCLEAR REALITY

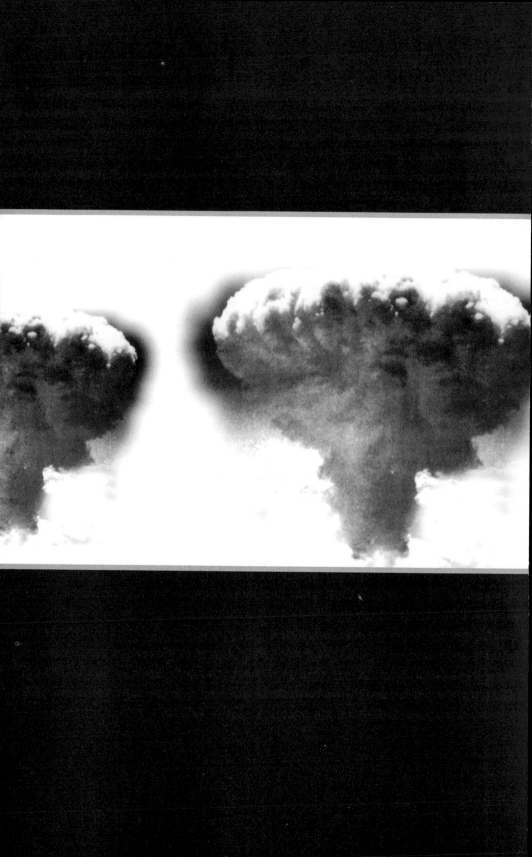

# THE NEW NUCLEAR REALITY

ELAINE LANDAU

TWENTY-FIRST CENTURY BOOKS
BROOKFIELD, CONNECTICUT

*To Derek Kessler*

Photographs courtesy of AP/Wide World Photos: pp. 2-3, 64; Rothco Cartoons: pp. 12 (© Schwadron), 29 (© Wicks/*The Signal*, CA), 41 (© Blower/*London Evening Standard*); Los Alamos National Laboratory: p. 14; © 1998 James Hill/NYT Pictures: p. 24; Senator Richard Lugar: p. 32; Reuters/Archive Photos: pp. 37 (© Mal Langsdon), 58 (© Mona Sharaf); Liaison Agency: pp. 44 (© Scott Peterson), 101 (top © Remi Benali; bottom © Bill Swersey); Corbis/AFP: p. 69; ISIS/IAEA: p. 84; Photofest: p. 90; © 1996 Kenneth Jarecke/Contact Press Images: p. 95

Library of Congress Cataloging-in-Publication Data
Landau, Elaine.
The new nuclear reality/Elaine Landau.
p. cm.
Includes bibliographical references and index.
ISBN 0-7613-1555-1 (lib. bdg.)
1. Nuclear weapons–Juvenile literature. 2. World politics–1989–Juvenile literature. 3. Nuclear arms control–Juvenile literature. [l. Nuclear arms control. 2. World politics. 3. Nuclear weapons.] I. Title
U264 .L36 2000
327.1'747–dc21          99-040023          CIP   AC

Published by Twenty-First Century Books
A Division of The Millbrook Press, Inc.
2 Old New Milford Road
Brookfield, Connecticut 06804
www.millbrookpress.com

# CONTENTS

# THE NEW NUCLEAR REALITY

# 1
## A NEW NUCLEAR REALITY

Picture this:

Suddenly there's a deafening explosion and a cloud of dust and extremely hot gases forms. In under a second the hot gases expand, creating a gigantic moving wall called a shock wave. The shock wave moves forward with incredible speed—in less than a minute it travels over 10 miles (16 kilometers), destroying most buildings in its path. Turbulent winds blow at speeds of about 400 miles (640 kilometers) per hour—much faster than the worst hurricane gusts ever experienced on Earth.

Thousands die immediately and many who survive suffer serious eye injuries and painful skin burns known as flash burns. Even people 10 miles from the blast have skin blisters. Anything flammable—dry leaves, stacks of newspapers, bales of hay—ignites, causing huge spreading fires that continue burning.

It's hard for anyone to escape the blast's effects since the explosion creates a huge mushroom-shaped cloud of radioactive material that emits high levels of radiation. Radiation destroys human cells as well as prevents cells from reproducing normally. A large dose of radiation will kill you. The particles from the mushroom-shaped cloud eventually land on the ground, rocks, and water, damaging living things over a broad area for years to come.

You've just read a description of a nuclear bomb explosion. If it sounds horrifying remember that a blast from some of today's large and enhanced nuclear bombs would be far worse. It's a frightening scenario, but not an unrealistic one.

The effects of a nuclear attack were experienced in Japan during World War II. In 1945 the United States, the first country to develop a nuclear bomb, dropped two over the Japanese cities of Hiroshima and Nagasaki. The devastating results ironically set the stage for the further development of these weapons of mass destruction (WMD). As the only nuclear power, the United States felt its enemies would be too afraid of the consequences to attack. But it wasn't long before other nations realized the deterrent value of nuclear weapons and wanted them as well. In 1949 the former Soviet Union became the second country to develop a nuclear bomb.

In the years that followed the United States and the Soviet Union engaged in an escalating arms race during which the two nations built and stockpiled an ever increasing number of nuclear weapons and delivery systems. Both needed to be certain that the fear of retaliation was too great for either to ever go to war. This period of heightened rivalry and suspiciousness between the United States and the Soviet Union and their allies was called the Cold War. It lasted almost fifty years, during which time the United States spent over $4 trillion to amass an enormous store of nuclear weapons.

Though historians agree that there were some close calls after Hiroshima and Nagasaki, these lethal weapons were never used again. The two superpowers developed an effective system of checks and balances. The standoff was scary but fairly stable, and as China, France, and Britain developed nuclear weapons the situation remained so. There were five declared nuclear powers and for years other nations chose to rely on the protection of one of them rather than develop their own nuclear arsenals.

However, this is hardly the case today. In 1974, India conducted nuclear tests; a few years later, U.S. intelligence learned that Israel was working on nuclear weaponry as well. Both of these countries had experienced conflicts with surrounding nations who were also becoming interested in gaining the military advantage of being a nuclear power.

Past nuclear stability was further threatened with the breakup of the Soviet Union in 1990. The large intimidating superstructure was gone but its nuclear capacity was not. Now the weapons were in the hands of newly independent countries—nations that were the fractured remains of a totalitarian superpower. While these countries may have lacked political and economic stability, they became instant nuclear powers nonetheless.

Unfortunately, such situations are less unique than many would like to believe. Nations in various parts of the world have set their sights on becoming nuclear powers even when in some cases much of the population lives in poverty. Although a country might need some help to develop its nuclear capability, the more nuclear states there are, the more available outside technical assistance becomes. New improved technology has made it easier for countries to

*A cartoonist takes nuclear proliferation to the ultimate degree—
Monaco and Luxembourg are two of the world's tiniest nations,
both nestled in the heart of Europe.*

create nuclear arsenals as well. It is likely that technologies developed for other purposes, such as lasers, will eventually make building a nuclear weapon both easier and less costly.

While decades ago information on building a nuclear bomb was considered top secret, much of this data is readily available today. Many libraries have a copy of the classic Los Alamos Primer: *First Lectures on How to Build an Atomic Bomb*. This isn't a step-by-step manual but it nevertheless offers valuable information on the physics of nuclear fission. Perhaps not coincidentally a copy of this manual was discovered in Iraqi leader Saddam Hussein's bomb development team's library.

Most physicists agree that there are no longer many secrets in atomic science in this age of information. As Terry Hawkins, deputy director of the nonproliferation and international security division of Los Alamos National Laboratory (where the first atom bombs were built) acknowledged, "There is a lot more information in the public domain that was not there ten years ago."[1]

Fearing condemnation and reprisals, some nations have initiated their bomb building efforts secretly. Therefore the international community has often had to rely on satellite information and intelligence sources to try to piece together a precise picture of a country's nuclear growth. The situation is highly fluid as well, since in some instances a change in government has either sped up or slowed down work on nuclear projects.

With a larger number of nations developing smaller nuclear weapons stashes, the nature of the risk changes from when the huge nuclear arsenals of the United States and the former Soviet Union were pitted against each other. At that time the nuclear stockpiles of either country were large enough to annihilate a significant percentage of the world's population. While the chances of such an occurrence may have decreased, some defense experts argue that the odds of a far lesser nuclear exchange may have increased.

The thought of a hostile nation or one run by a ruthless dictator with access to nuclear weapons may be especially unsettling. However, some individuals argue that we need to look at the broader picture. They stress that it is unfair to

Robert Oppenheimer directed the laboratory at Los Alamos, New Mexico, where the first atomic bomb was designed and built. Oppenheimer and his colleagues were enthused and idealistic about their quest to develop an atomic bomb before Nazi Germany. He was to report later, "Almost everyone knew that this job, if it were achieved, would be part of history. The sense of excitement, of devotion and of patriotism in the end prevailed." Indeed it did. Oppenheimer would ever after be known as the "father of the atomic bomb."

classify some nations as "rogue" states while the United States still maintains its supply of nuclear weapons. Questioning the accepted wisdom that nuclear weapons are safe and desirable when controlled by "responsible" nations, while reminding us of Hiroshima and Nagasaki, they have called for the total abolition of all nuclear armaments. Yet things appear to be heading in the opposite direction as nuclear proliferation continues in many parts of the world.

Another threatening prospect on the horizon is that of nuclear weapons falling into the hands of terrorist groups. There are many issues to deal with, but one thing is certain—containing the nuclear threat has never been more challenging, as the world comes to grip with the new nuclear reality.

# 2
## THE SITUATION IN RUSSIA

When the former Soviet empire abruptly collapsed in 1990, many Americans breathed a sigh of relief. The danger of the United States being demolished by a foreign nuclear superpower seemed distantly remote at that point. However, the Soviet Union's dissolution into a number of smaller poorly prepared republics and the serious economic difficulties they've experienced resulted in a whole new set of unexpected problems regarding nuclear weapons security. Problems that could easily have worldwide consequences.

Department of Energy secretary Bill Richardson succinctly summed up the dilemma when he said, "Nobody anticipated that the Russian economy would be in such bad shape."[1] Yet it is. About 70 percent of all Russians are barely surviving near or below the subsistence level. More than 40 million exist under the official poverty line, with so many elderly pensioners dying of starvation that these stories are not even considered news anymore.

The Russian government's yearly revenues are less than what the U.S. Treasury receives in just one week. Consequently the government in Russia is unable to pay much of its workforce, including nuclear scientists, soldiers guarding nuclear sites, and many others involved with nuclear materials and weapons at varying levels. In some cases the heat has even been turned off in buildings where nuclear materials are stored because the government cannot pay its electric bill. Even more distressing is the fact that electrically powered security systems on these facilities have been shut off on occasion.

The situation may have hit near bottom in August 1998 when Russian defense minister Igor Sergeyev ordered all military officers to "look for additional sources [of food for the winter] and assume personal control."[2] Shortly afterward the Defense Ministry organized trips to the countryside during which army officers and rank-and-file soldiers were taken out to fields and forested areas to forage for nuts, berries, mushrooms, and any other food supplies that could keep them alive through the winter. The implication of these events is sobering. Russian military personnel weren't just going on nature walks—they were leaving nuclear facilities unguarded while they gathered berries to keep from starving in the months ahead.

Under these circumstances it's not surprising that in some cases the military has resorted to desperate measures, opening the door to some potentially high risk situations. The following are just a sample of the lapses in nuclear security that can occur with a demoralized population in an economically devastated country.

• When Russian nuclear workers protested not receiving wages for months, the Russian minister of atomic energy Eugeniy Adamov announced that the government owed the ministry over $170 million and hadn't paid a cent in over two months. Nevertheless, the protests continued with more than 47,000 workers from the nuclear sector participating in demonstrations at designated locations throughout the country. The nuclear workers' trade union claimed that over $400 million in back wages was owed to nuclear workers who were sorely in need of the funds. If these workers aren't paid soon, might they be tempted to sell nuclear materials or expertise to unauthorized outside sources?

• Five soldiers at a Russian nuclear weapons test area—the 12th Main Directorate at Novaya Zemiya—killed a guard before taking another guard hostage and removing what was believed to be a container of nuclear material. The small band hoped to hijack a plane to make their getaway but fortunately were apprehended by authorities first.

• A nineteen-year-old Russian sailor aboard a nuclear-attack submarine reached his breaking point and engaged in a crazed killing spree on the vessel. He attacked and killed a sentry with a chisel before murdering another seven of his shipmates with an AK-47. He then locked himself in the torpedo bay, where he threatened to use the nuclear reactor to blow up the submarine. The youth ended the frightening scenario by taking his own life, leaving the international community considerably shaken by the narrowly averted disaster.

"The country was on the verge of a nuclear catastrophe," Vladmir Prikhodko, the regional director of Russia's Federal Security Service told *The Washington Post*. "If the sailor . . . blew up the munitions stored [on the sub], we would have had a second Chernobyl."[3] His sentiments were echoed by former Russian Navy captain Alexander Nikitin, who said in *The Toronto Star*, "It is really scary that one day the use of nuclear arms may depend on the sentiments of someone who is feeling blue, who got out of bed on the wrong side and does not feel like living."[4]

• A U.S. team of nuclear scientists and physicists visited Moscow's Kurchutov Institute, where 100 kilograms of nuclear materials—enough to make several bombs—were being housed. Since the institute didn't have funding to pay $50 a week for a guard, the facility was left unguarded.

• A report from Russia's Chief Military Prosecutor's Office indicated that out of the various military divisions, crime was most prevalent in the country's Strategic Rocket Forces—the unit handling nuclear weapons. The incidence of crime had risen a full 25 percent from 1996 to 1997. The division's vulnerability was further revealed when over twenty men in the Strategic Rocket Forces were discharged from the service for serious psychiatric disorders. A number of those let go were guards at nuclear arsenals.

It's difficult not to be concerned about the state of nuclear weapons in Russia. Despite numerous attempts at arms reduction through the years, the nation still has over 20,000 nuclear weapons housed in more than ninety installations throughout the country. Russia's total arsenal includes thousands of small tactical nuclear weapons and 6,250 deployed long-range missile and bomber weapons. A large number of these weapons systems are still on alert and could be launched with just fifteen minutes' warning.

Russia's severe economic problems and subsequent government budget cuts have made it increasingly difficult for the country to maintain and replace key systems necessary to safeguard nuclear facilities. Often these "at risk" situations involve entire communities, as the vital centers of Russia's industrial-military complex have generally been hidden away in closed cities in Siberia or other distant regions far from the country's capital. There are at least ten of these secret Russian cities—home to about 750,000 people. Usually, these places have only been referred to by code names such as Chelyabinsk-65, Sverdlousk-45, or Krasnoyarsk-26.

Reporters from the United States only recently gained entry to Krasnoyarsk-26, a city the Central Intelligence Agency (CIA) had been anxious to inspect for over four decades. In many ways, Krasnoyarsk-26 is typical of the Russian secret cities where nuclear weapons are designed and manufactured. Although over 100,000 people live there, Krasnoyarsk-26 can't be found on any map and most Russians don't even know it exists.

Krasnoyarsk-26 is a city built within a mountain to insure that it is completely hidden from view. It can only be reached by a single rail line that runs through a maze of dark twisting mountain tunnels. Its residents were invited to live there by the government, but after arriving they were not permitted to leave or have visitors from the outside. Although the people living there have phones, they were only allowed to make calls within the city, and even these communications were monitored.

The city has been there since the 1950s but no one was ever supposed to even suspect that a thriving metropolis existed within a mountain in Siberia. That's because its sole purpose for being there was to produce substantial quantities of nuclear materials—more than enough to eradicate the entire United States.

Through the years the CIA had tried to learn more about Krasnoyarsk-26 by studying satellite camera images

*The city of Krasnoyarsk-26 lies at the end of a three-mile (5-km) tunnel, shown here under construction, leading to the interior of a mountain. Because the subterranean city did not appear on a map, it got its name from the number on the post office box in the real city of Krasnoyarsk, 40 miles (65 km) south of the mountain, where its citizens' mail was sent.*

and noting telltale landscape changes. The organization knew that nuclear weapons were being produced at the site because the solidly frozen Yenisei River melted as it neared the city. This meant that large quantities of hot steamy water were flowing into the river and that hot water had to be produced by nuclear reactors and plutonium.

The former Soviet Union erected this city during the Cold War to advance its weapons program. The only reason that Krasnoyarsk-26 and other secret cities existed was to manufacture nuclear weapons as well as the plutonium and highly enriched uranium necessary to create these weapons of mass destruction. Top nuclear scientists from different parts of the country along with experienced nuclear workers were recruited for Krasnoyarsk-26, where so far 40 tons of plutonium, which is enough to make ten thousand nuclear bombs, has been generated.

Initially Krasnoyarsk-26 offered its residents quite a luxurious lifestyle. The nuclear scientists and engineers and their families lived in lovely residences on a street named Nobility Row, and while Russians in most cities waited for hours on line for rations, there were no food or clothing shortages in this hidden mountain city. Those living there always had the best of everything. The food available to them was so varied, plentiful, and fresh that Krasnoyarsk-26ers were nicknamed "the chocolate eaters."[5] They could also buy stylish clothing unavailable to others and were given free tickets to Krasnoyarsk-26's theater and opera. The major drawback to living there was the ever-present threat of a deadly radiation leak. Instead of a town clock at the center of this metropolis, there's a Geiger counter.

About a half mile into the mountain lies the control room for Krasnoyarsk-26's three nuclear reactors. During the Cold War all three nuclear reactors were functioning at full capacity to produce plutonium. Yet more than a decade after the Cold War ended, one of Krasnoyarsk-26's reactors is still actively manufacturing this deadly nuclear material.

The nuclear reactor annually produces a half ton of plutonium, enough to create about one hundred nuclear bombs. Plutonium may look like a harmless paste, but its appearance does not make it any less deadly. If you're wondering why the last reactor at Krasnoyarsk-26 has not been turned off, there's a simple answer. If it were, the approximately 100,000 people living in this icy cold Siberian city would freeze to death. That's because besides making plutonium, the nuclear reactor is used to heat the city. The reactors are connected to a gigantic boiler room about the length of two football fields that furnishes steam to a system of above-ground pipes running throughout the city.

The recent economic hardships affecting the rest of Russia have also been keenly felt in this nuclear city and others like it. When in July 1998, Vice President Al Gore visited the nuclear city of Arzamas-16 (now known as Sarov) thousands of nuclear scientists were on strike to protest the drop in their standard of living and months of not being paid for their work. The situation is similar in Krasnoyarsk-26, where the people once known as the chocolate eaters no longer have very much to eat.

According to Joseph Cirincione, director of the nonproliferation project at the Carnegie Endowment for International Peace in Washington, D.C., "Tens of thousands of nuclear scientists [in the former Soviet Union] are seriously underpaid and increasingly desperate."[6] These individuals could be ripe candidates for amply budgeted nuclear pro-

*This photograph of Krasnoyarsk-26 today accompanied a November 1998 New York Times article depicting the economic hardship that hit the once economically privileged city when two of its three nuclear reactors shut down.*

grams in Iraq, Iran, and other countries interested in securing nuclear expertise to have their own nuclear weapons arsenals. Senior Ukrainian officials have already told U.S. political analysts in Washington, D.C., "that they know of many scientists who have given up hope of working again in their country and have left for jobs in other countries, including Iraq."[7]

As economic and political conditions crumble in the former Soviet Union, the military's access to and control over nuclear weapons becomes comparably frightening. The Center for Defense Intelligence in the United States has underscored that "crime, violence, and corruption flourish within the [Russian] military" noting that "of particular concern is the fact that there are thousands of nuclear weapons in the hands of a demoralized and underpaid military."[8]

Aleksandr Lebed, governor of Siberia's Krasnoyarsk region and a retired general, warned President Clinton during his visit to Russia that the situation in his country has dangerously escalated and that the ultimate consequences could surpass those of the Russian Revolution. "The situation is worse than in 1917," Lebed said. "Now we have huge stockpiles of poorly guarded nuclear weapons."[9]

Lebed has firsthand knowledge of the incipient crisis. At one point he wrote to the Russian prime minister to say that if the situation deteriorated any further in the region in which he was governor, he would be tempted to take over the nuclear weapons housed there as a bargaining chip. Describing the officers in a nuclear unit within his jurisdiction as "hungry and angry," Lebed wrote, "I am seriously thinking of establishing territorial jurisdiction over it [the nuclear arsenal]. We in Krasnoyarsk are not rich yet, but in exchange for the status of a nuclear territory, we could feed [our soldiers] and become a headache for the world community along with India and Pakistan."[10]

Under these circumstances it's not unreasonable to think that a desperate, hungry soldier with access to a nuclear facility might sneak a few handfuls of uranium to sell to the highest bidder. Some soldiers have already been caught selling conventional (nonnuclear) weapons and ammunition to buy food or liquor. Even rank-and-file Russian soldiers seem to expect it to happen as they watch the morale and hopes of the men they work with reach new lows. "It is pretty reckless on the part of [Russian president Boris] Yeltsin . . . to entrust these weapons to youths who are suffering malnutrition, cold and neglect by their commanders," one Russian soldier pointed out.[11]

A scoop of highly enriched uranium about the size of a softball would be sufficient to create a nuclear bomb. Of course, it takes more than highly enriched uranium and plutonium to make a nuclear weapon. But Matthew Bunn, a former advisor to the White House Office of Science and Technology Policy and a member of the Russian-American Nuclear Security Advisory Council (RANSAC), notes that "by far, the hardest part of making a nuclear bomb is getting hold of the plutonium. And once you have the material you're 80 to 90 percent of the way there to having a nuclear bomb."[12]

Possibly a terrorist group could break into one of the inadequately secured Russian nuclear warehouses and steal enough uranium for a small arsenal of nuclear weapons. Worse yet, if Russia's economic predicament further disintegrated, might the government be willing to sell sizable amounts of its nuclear materials to secure the necessary funds to hold the nation together? Intelligence sources have shown that there is no shortage of buyers for nuclear materials. "We know for a fact that Iran sent agents to Russia looking for the technologies of advanced weapons, and that some Russian institutes were willing to sell," Matthew Bunn cited.[13] There's further evidence that following the Gulf War, even when U.N. inspectors searched possible weapons facilities in Iraq, Saddam Hussein sent Iraqi officials to Russia to look into purchasing nuclear materials and nuclear weapons delivery systems. In addition, it's been rumored that Libya will pay a large amount of money to Russia or anyone else who can sell and deliver a sufficient quantity of plutonium to them.

In a climate of economic, political, and social unrest anything is possible. As Department of Energy secretary Bill Richardson put it, "If you asked me what threatens the average American the most in the world, it's no longer the threat of the big Russian bear with nuclear weapons aimed at us. What it is now is those Russian weapons and expertise and materials being stolen and used by states like Iraq, like Iran, like North Korea . . . that are ultimate enemies. That's the nightmare scenario that we're worried about . . . . And what is very dramatic also is that the supply at one Russian nuclear site, one of 10, [at] one of the biggest, there is more fissile material to make a nuclear weapon than in all the stockpiles of France, Great Britain, and China combined."[14]

The present nuclear problem in Russia was further detailed in a report by the National Research Council of the National Academy of Sciences, a U.S. government-chartered organization of top scientists. The report charged that less than 1 percent of the 1,500 tons of Russia's plutonium and highly enriched uranium that could be used to make atomic weapons by terrorists or "outlaw" nations is presently properly safeguarded.

The committee identified the two most troublesome areas as the inadequate security measures concerning Russian plutonium and uranium stocks and the weak controls on the export of nuclear technology. "In view of the extensive and often remote borders of the countries of the . . . [former Soviet Union] enforcement of export controls will be a difficult task," the report stated. "Significant transfers of sensitive items are a serious possibility."[15]

In describing the scope of the problem, the report added, "The challenge of controlling small amounts of [nuclear] material located in hundreds of buildings, including many in a poor state of repair, seems overwhelming."[16] Among the most frightening realities unearthed by the report was the acknowledgement by Russian officials that two dozen thefts and attempted thefts of nuclear materials had occurred. The situation becomes even more desperate, since in commenting on the current state of affairs in Russia, former CIA director John Deutch told a Senate investigative subcommittee, "The Russians may not even know where all their material is located."[17] That makes it all the more difficult to account for what may be missing.

Some instances of the theft or disappearance of Russian nuclear materials have been highly publicized. One such case occurred in May 1993, when thirty-three crates of highly enriched uranium mixed with a metal substance were uncovered in a bank vault in Vilnius, Lithuania. It had been shipped there from a Russian physics institute by a company called AMI–which was actually the name of a cover operation for two Russian middlemen. If the scheme had worked, the crates would have been picked up by organized crime figures in Lithuania and eventually sent to the Middle East. An investigation revealed that a senior

*A 1992 Wicks cartoon sums up the U.S. fear of nuclear weapons in the hands of Russia and the other countries that were once part of the Soviet Union. Unsavory-looking representatives of some of the nations that spawn terrorism are lined up, ready to offer a bag of cash to the newly formed countries that need money far more than they need nuclear capability.*

regional Russian government official as well as a high-ranking officer at a nuclear storage facility were involved. While the amount smuggled through was insufficient for a bomb, this route could have been used for larger quantities at a later time.

The same year 4 kilograms of enriched uranium were stolen from a Russian naval shipyard by second-class Russian Navy captain Alexei Tikhomirov. Feeling desperate with nowhere to turn, Tikhomirov had broken through a wooden fence and sawed off the padlock on the warehouse door where the nuclear fuel was kept. Mikhail Kulick, the head Russian investigator on the case, wasn't surprised that the robbery occurred and commented in an interview,"Potatoes are better guarded."[18]

The sale of accompanying delivery systems for nuclear weapons presents a problem as well. In 1997, five assault transport helicopters equipped with weapons pods capable of carrying nuclear bombs were stopped by Russian customs officers on their way to North Korea. Stolen by Russian military officers, these military aircraft were valued at $300,000 each but had been sold by the desperate men for just $20,000 apiece.

The U.S. Central Intelligence Agency (CIA) also found that a number of gyroscopes–the core of a military missile's guidance system–were missing from a number of recently dismantled Russian missiles. Since gyroscopes are crucial to a ballistic missile accurately striking its target, their sale is severely restricted. Through informants it was learned that the missing gyroscopes were stored in a shed in Jordan's Amman airport before they were to be sent on to Iraq. Jordan's former King Hussein was notified and the gyroscopes were seized and promptly turned over to the United Nations.

Since that time it's been revealed that other gyroscopes from Russian missiles were already shipped to a major missile research facility outside Baghdad. As these gyroscopes can be used in missiles carrying nuclear warheads the situation is serious, but unfortunately the smugglers weren't caught. "Someone in Russia knew that the gyroscopes were not well protected and that person was able to contact the Iraqis and make a deal," offered Leonard Spector, director of nonproliferation and arms control at the Department of Energy. "Very likely, there are other pipelines in place to other rogue countries or terrorist groups. And if gyroscopes can pass along a pipeline, so can weapons-grade materials."[19]

U.S. leaders are well aware that Russia's problems have ramifications for the United States and much of the rest of the world. As President Bill Clinton said in New York on September 14, 1998, in an address to the Council on Foreign Relations,"Russia is facing an economic crisis that threatens the extraordinary progress the Russian people have made in just seven years, building a new society from the ground up. . . . At worst, adversity in Russia could affect not only the Russian economy and prospects for our economic cooperation—it could also have an impact on our cooperation with Russia on nuclear disarmament, on fighting terrorism, and the spread of weapons of mass destruction, on standing together for peace, from the Balkans to the Middle East."[20]

As early as 1991, when the Soviet Union broke up, President George Bush reached out to Russia to offer aid for political and economic reform as well as assistance in controlling and reducing their nuclear stockpiles. The U.S. Congress speedily approved programs toward this end. A giant step forward was the bipartisan Cooperative Threat Reduction (CTR) program, also known as the "Nunn-Lugar" program for former Democratic senator Sam Nunn and Republican senator Richard Lugar, who joined forces to design it. Created to deal with the Cold War's dangerous nuclear legacy, the program provided funds and assistance to Russia in corralling nuclear weap-

U.S. senators Richard Lugar (far left) and Sam Nunn (second from left) join Ukrainian officials in the town of Derazhnya in central Ukraine in a farewell look at a missile silo shortly before destroying it. The 1996 destruction took place as a part of the CTR nuclear reduction program sponsored by the senators.

ons from the various former Soviet republics into Russia's domain. The program also helped in dismantling nuclear weapons pointed at the United States, reducing stockpiles and safeguarding and accounting for leftover nuclear materials.

To counter the threat of unpaid and demoralized Russian nuclear scientists selling their skills or nuclear technology to hostile third parties, CTR was expanded both in scope and funding. Money was allotted to put Russian nuclear scientists to work researching how to best transport, store, and dismantle nuclear weapons. In other instances Nunn-Lugar funding was used as seed money to convert weapons machinery and installations to manufacturing plants for dental equipment, hearing aids, and soda bottling operations.

So far, CTR has achieved a great deal. The former Soviet republics of Ukraine, Belarus, and Kazakhstan are no longer nuclear states and in compliance with CTR have turned over all their nuclear weapons to Russia. In at least one especially dramatic endeavor, nuclear material was taken from these locations and brought to the United States for safekeeping. That was the essence of "Project Sapphire," a top secret operation carried out in Kazakhstan that arranged for the safe transport of 600 kilograms of highly enriched uranium to a secure facility in Oak Ridge, Tennessee. As Secretary of Defense William Perry noted, "Without our cooperation with Kazakhstan on Nunn-Lugar, we might have never known about the existence of this material."[21]

According to the Center for Defense Intelligence, the following Russian nuclear weapons and delivery systems have already been destroyed: 339 ballistic missiles, 286 ballistic missile launchers, and 30 submarine-launched ballistic missiles. Perhaps most importantly, 4,838 warheads on strategic systems pointed at the United States have been deactivated. In 1998 the U.S. Department of Energy started still another Russian-based nuclear safety program called the Second Line of Defense. The goal of this endeavor is to help the Russian government stop the theft of nuclear material and technology from its borders, but as Russia is the world's largest country, this has been quite a challenge.

While still in office, President Bush worked with Russian president Boris Yeltsin on arms reduction treaties. In January 1993 both presidents signed START II (the second Strategic Arms Reduction Treaty) to dramatically reduce the number of long-range nuclear weapons in both countries' arsenals. Although the U.S. Congress ratified START II in 1996, the Russian Duma (the lower house of Russia's Parliament) hasn't done so as of yet.

The reason for its lack of action is twofold. Of course, putting the treaty into effect would be quite costly, but the second reason is the overall erosion of much of the goodwill between the United States and Russia that existed in the early 1990s. There had been a wonderful period of hope in U.S.-Russian relations from about 1992 to 1993. But before long some in the Russian government began to feel that the United States now treated their nation like a country defeated in war rather than one going through a difficult transition. In Russia's Parliament some officials accused the United States of trying to take unfair advantage of their nation when it was at its weakest.

The Russians had also grown extremely wary of the continued growth of the North Atlantic Treaty Organization (NATO)—a military alliance consisting of the United

States and fifteen other nations. NATO began in 1949, largely as a way for European nations to guard against an attack by the powerful former Soviet Union. All NATO nations agreed to vigorously defend an attack against any member nation. But the United States was always the most important part of NATO because of its superior military strength and nuclear weapons. Member nations felt that the former Soviet Union would not attack them because of possible U.S. nuclear retaliation.

With the fall of the former Soviet government, ideally there should have been no further need for NATO. Yet instead of folding, there's been a U.S.-led expansion of the alliance, making the Russians feel that their nation is still regarded as a threat rather than as a new partner in insuring Europe's safety. With so many countries allied against it, some Russian officials also fear that the United States and its NATO allies might someday take military action or use the threat of military force against their country.

They've grown especially concerned about what they perceived as an increasing tendency by the United States to resort to military force without first consulting Russia. These include U.S. assaults on suspected terrorist facilities in Afghanistan and Africa as well as the attacks on Libya in 1993, on Bosnia in 1994, and on Iraq in 1995, 1996, and 1998. Russia has also expressed the fear that in significantly reducing its nuclear arsenal, the United States hopes to keep their country weakened as a permanent second-rate power.

An even further deterioration in U.S.-Russian relations resulted as a rivalry between the nations developed over the oil and natural gas reserves in the Caspian Sea region. The United States sees these natural resources as potential development opportunities for U.S. companies as well as a way to enhance and diversify its own supply sources. The Russians, on the other hand, view the region as long being within their country's sphere of influence and fear that U.S. investment there may lessen available Western financial backing for Russian oil production in Siberia and Far East Russia. This uneasiness was compounded by the Pentagon's 1994 Nuclear Posture Review, which underscored the continuing need for U.S. reliance on nuclear weapons as a vital part of its military defense system.

All these factors significantly slowed down U.S.-Russian cooperation on nonproliferation treaties and nuclear arms reduction, adding to the unstable conditions presently existing in Russia. Some feel that it's up to the United States to take the initiative in finding a solution. This was the position advocated by the Committee on Nuclear Policy, a coalition of arms control and research groups that issued a 1999 report urging the administration to more vigorously pursue arms control negotiations with Russia.

The committee believes that the United States is missing an important opportunity to introduce new nuclear disarmament measures by waiting for the Russian Parliament to ratify START II. "To continue to rely solely on the stalemated START II process is to needlessly increase the costs and risks of maintaining U.S. and Russian nuclear arsenals at levels well in excess of what is needed to deter an attack," the report stated.[22]

The document further stressed that the risk of a nuclear action would be sharply reduced if both the United States and Russia immediately began to reduce their nuclear stockpiles so that each country had no more than a total of one thousand nuclear weapons–including both strategic and battlefield warheads. This would be a dramatic change from

Former U.S. president George Bush and then Soviet President Mikhail Gorbachev are shown here exchanging pens after signing START II in January 1993. The U.S. Congress ratified the agreement to reduce the number of long-range nuclear weapons in both countries' arsenals in 1996, but the Russian Duma has yet to do so, prompting pressure on the U.S. to unilaterally disarm.

how things were at the height of the Cold War, when the United States and the former Soviet Union had over ten thousand nuclear warheads apiece. The report also suggests that the two sides continue to take additional missiles off alert status as well as eradicate options in their war plans for a massive nuclear attack.

The committee believes that if the Russians won't take the necessary steps, the United States should unilaterally begin the vital reductions. The report pointed out that in 1991, President George Bush unilaterally removed tactical nuclear weapons from overseas bases and from surface ships. He also took a thousand nuclear warheads off B-52 bombers and removed a large number of missiles from alert status. In turn, Russian president Mikhail Gorbachev responded by paving the way for dramatic nuclear arms reductions in his country.

Although the Committee on Nuclear Policy includes such distinguished experts as former Secretary of Defense Robert S. McNamara and General Andrew J. Goodpaster, a former NATO commander, the White House issued a statement indicating that it will not be following the committee's proposed guidelines. Robert G. Bell, special assistant to the president for defense policy and arms control at the National Security Council, described the report's recommendations as "well intended" but more than the administration was willing to do. "At the end of the day, the proposals are too ambitious and too idealistic," Bell stated.[23] As Russia and the United States continue to blame each other for the impasse, it's clear that there are no easy answers.

# 3

## THE MIDDLE EAST:
## IRAQ, IRAN, LIBYA, AND ISRAEL

The Middle East has long been a hotbed of tumultuous politics and border disputes. When nuclear weapons are added to the equation, the potential for deadly violence in the region skyrockets. One particularly troublesome spot in the area is Iraq, where Saddam Hussein is attempting to build a nuclear arsenal along with other weapons of mass destruction.

Following Iraq's August 1990 invasion of Kuwait and its subsequent defeat in the Gulf War, Hussein had to deal with United Nations-imposed sanctions as well as inspections of possible weapons sites by the United Nations Special Commission on Iraq (UNSCOM) and the International Atomic Energy Agency (IAEA). Experts felt that the inspections were crucial since it was learned that by 1990, following an intensive weapons buildup, Iraq was thought to be only about six months away from having a nuclear bomb.

Yet at the time no one knew how successful the inspectors would be against Saddam Hussein, who was determined to thwart their efforts from the start. Initially the Iraqi government denied having a nuclear weapons program or ever having had one for that matter. Officials claimed that any nuclear weapons plans attributed to their country were nothing more than vicious rumors spread by the United States to ruin Iraq's image as a peace-seeking nation.

However, when U.N. inspectors found and seized papers indicating the contrary, the Iraqis finally owned up to having a nuclear weapons program. "They could not argue with the documents," one U.N. inspector on the team explained.[1] As Richard Butler, Australian diplomat and executive chairman of UNSCOM, described Saddam Hussein's tactics, "From the beginning, Saddam Hussein refused to tell the truth. He created a top level committee to conceal weapons–to bury them, to hide them, to move them around the country in the dead of night so that we would never find them. For every member of UNSCOM in the field, the Iraqis have dedicated ten [workers] to frustrating his work. We've had to reject their disclosures. We've had to reconstruct bits of exploded weapons like jigsaw puzzle pieces in the desert."[2]

Saddam Hussein has also found ways around the economic sanctions to finance his nuclear work. Although U.N. sanctions only permit Iraq to export oil in return for food and other humanitarian goods, Saddam managed to sell oil for sizable profits in the United Arab Emirates. The smuggled-out oil was shipped through Iranian waters and across the narrow Strait of Hormuz.

U.S. Fifth Fleet ships patrol the Gulf and routinely stop suspicious vessels to inspect their cargo but these patrols are barred from entering Iranian waters. According to recent estimates as much as 20 percent of low-grade oil from the Persian Gulf originates in Iraq. "With these funds the

*A London cartoon pokes fun at the effectiveness of the U.N. inspections in Iraq, an operation in which Great Britain participated. Saddam Hussein is shown welcoming the inspectors to the front door of a facility, while a truck full of missiles is exiting the back door.*

Iraqis have [had]. . . significant windows of opportunity for engaging in prohibited activities at new sites," noted foreign analyst Patrick Clawson of the Washington Institute on Near East Policy.[3]

As time passed and the sanctions and inspections continued, the Iraqis became increasingly proficient at concealing contraband materials and documents revealing current nuclear weapons development. In 1998 continual interference with UNSCOM and IAEA inspectors prevented the team from effectively doing their job for nearly seven out of twelve months. "UNSCOM has had great successes, but lately, there have been diminishing returns," Anthony H. Cordesman, a nuclear expert at the Center for Strategic and International Studies in Washington, D.C., confirmed at the time.[4]

Then at the end of October 1998, Iraq flatly refused to cooperate any further with UNSCOM, risking a military strike from the United States and Britain, which still had forces on alert in the Persian Gulf. Iraq was warned that only its full cooperation with UNSCOM inspectors could avert military action. At first it looked as though Saddam Hussein might relent under pressure, but soon afterward Iraq's foreign minister Mohammed Saled al-Sahhaf formally rebuffed the U.N.'s demand for additional documentation on the country's weapons program. He claimed that Iraq had already given the U.N. more than enough files and had nothing left to turn over.

The Iraqi response set the stage for the mid-December 1998 air strike known as Operation Desert Fox in which 280 American cruise missiles hit Iraq with an intensity reminiscent of the Gulf War. The military targets included six suspected nuclear weapons sites and five potential chemical or biological weapons facilities. "We are delivering a message," President Clinton told Iraq and the rest of the world on December 16, 1998, ". . . if you act recklessly, you will pay."[5]

The goal of the U.S.-British air assault was to destroy or at least severely disrupt Saddam Hussein's ability to amass weapons of mass destruction, and following the four-day attack, President Clinton proclaimed, "I am confident that we have achieved our mission."[6] The Pentagon reported that over one hundred targets were struck. U.S. defense secretary William Cohen noted that Saddam Hussein's weapons delivery systems and his military command control centers were among those most severely hit, adding that Hussein's guided missile program had been set back a year. The American public was shown satellite photos of the bombed remains of Saddam Hussein's military intelligence headquarters and missile bases, but the defense secretary admitted that the missile attacks failed to significantly harm Iraqi nuclear weapons production sites–largely because United Nations inspectors had been unable to unearth the still secret locations of many of these facilities.

In the final analysis, the air campaign probably resulted in more of a temporary setback for the Iraqi dictator than a decisive blow to his weapons production ability. Despite tremendous odds, Saddam Hussein has shown himself to be incredibly resilient in the past and so far there is no reason to believe he won't continue to be. "He [Iraqi President Saddam Hussein] is going to rebuild," predicted General Bindford Peay III, a former U.S. Army commander in the Gulf who worked on the initial plans for the air attack on Iraq. "It will certainly take a few years. With this [the air strikes], we're just buying some time."[7]

Yet even though the military action might have delayed Saddam Hussein a bit, some feel that in the long run the endeavor could have actually hurt rather than helped the ultimate objective. There are those who believe that despite the many obstacles U.N. inspectors had to deal with, the inspections were still far more effective at hindering Iraq's nuclear development than military intervention. "I've walked every inch of those buildings [the Iraqi intelligence

*In December 1998, the nighttime sky above Baghdad was ablaze with lights from cruise missiles as American and British warplanes attacked a wide range of suspected Iraqi military installations after Iraq's refusal to cooperate with U.N. officials.*

headquarters and others hit in the air raids]," noted Scott Ritter, a former Marine who resigned as a U.N. weapons inspector, "and I know there was nothing of significance in there."[8]

With the military strike putting an end to U.N. inspections in Iraq, the United States and its allies will have to rely on less precise measures such as intelligence reports and satellite photos to learn of Iraq's future nuclear development. Meanwhile the December 1998 collision with the U.S. and British forces might have inadvertently served to bolster Hussein's image in the region. "Saddam Hussein can emerge as a hero who faced down U.S. imperialism," commented Hamid Bayati, spokesperson for the Islamic Revolution in Iraq. "He will attract more sympathy for Iraq among Muslims. Mounting the strikes without a [U.S.] political strategy to overthrow the regime could be counterproductive."[9]

Unfortunately, the bombing of Iraq was also viewed negatively by Russia and China, two other nuclear powers. The continued use of force by the United States in the Gulf region has sat especially poorly with Russia. Florida representative Porter Goss, chairman of the House Intelligence Committee, reported that Russia has threatened to halt its own nuclear arms reductions as long as U.S. relations with the Arab world continue to be strained. "The ripple effect [of the air strikes] is not very good," Goss said. "Our troops brilliantly executed their orders. But I think we've set ourselves back in almost every way we can. The one exception is that we've temporarily set him [Saddam Hussein] back on some capabilities." Goss added, "There's no policy here . . . this is just flip-flop adhockery."[10]

After demanding an end to the air strikes in the U.N. Security Council, Russia recalled its ambassadors from Washington and London. Those close to Russian president Boris Yeltsin said that he was so enraged by the military assault on Iraq that he initially refused to speak with anyone from the White House. China's president Jiang Zemin publicly denounced the bombings as well.

But besides the adverse reaction of some of the nuclear powers, relying on military means to contain Saddam Hussein's nuclear weapons growth has been costly in other ways. Nearly a quarter of a billion dollars was spent for the 320 ship-launched Tomahawks used in Desert Fox, while another ninety million was needed for the larger cruise missiles launched from B-52 bombers. And even prior to the air strikes, policing Iraqi nuclear development in 1998 alone cost over two billion dollars—that's twenty times the price of keeping a U.S. presence in the Gulf region the year following the Gulf War.

At this point there's no end in sight. At least 20,000 U.S. troops will remain as an ongoing presence in the region, trying to level Saddam Hussein's ability to generate weapons of mass destruction as the need arises. Pentagon experts acknowledge that in addition to the cost of deploying troops and weapons to the region, there's also the wear and tear on military equipment and troop morale to consider. Right now no one knows how long American soldiers and sailors will be there. One senior defense official who did not want to be identified reportedly confirmed that the situation could continue indefinitely. "Look at Fidel Castro," he noted.[11]

Yet despite the drawbacks and the monetary drain, there are those in the Defense Department who argue that this course of action is inexpensive compared to more drastic choices. They believe that these measures take a worse toll on the Iraqi dictator and his weapons buildup plans than may be realized. "This kind of punishment is comparatively cheap for us and it's not cheap for the Iraqis because of the [U.N.] sanctions," suggested retired General Michael Dugan, the former Air Force chief of staff who was instrumental in planning the Gulf War. "This is a holding action. . . . If you want to change the regime, you need to invade Iraq. And given that alternative, this is cheap."[12]

Nevertheless, the predicament in Iraq is becoming increasingly serious since Saddam Hussein appears bent on developing a nuclear arsenal and without U.N. inspections he has a freer hand to do so. Dealing with Hussein is especially unnerving for the international community since so often in the past he has gone back on his promises. Teams of U.N. negotiators have worked with him and his representatives reaching a variety of agreements only to find that they've been deceived. This means that the countries he's negotiated with never know where they really stand.

"Saddam Hussein represents the worst nightmare for the system," explained Richard Butler of UNSCOM. "He clearly wants to acquire illegal weapons of mass destruction. . . he abuses the system the international community has built. He signs all the treaties, then secretly pushes ahead with development. That distinguishes Iraq from those few countries that have persisted in developing their own nuclear weapons, in spite of the broad international consensus [against it]. At least, they don't sign treaties."[13]

Saddam Hussein's determination to amass a sizable nuclear arsenal became chillingly clear when a number of high-ranking Iraqi defectors from his regime revealed the steps already taken toward that goal. Among the most vocal of these individuals is Khidhir Hamza, an American-educated Iraqi scientist with degrees from both MIT and Florida State University who was formerly Iraq's director of nuclear weaponization.

Although Saddam Hussein has invested time and resources in also developing biological and chemical weapons, Hamza knows firsthand that the nuclear program is his top priority. ". . . There's a limit to what he can use the chemical for; the same for the biological," Hamza explained. "But the nuclear . . . he will be invincible with that. He'll be the hero of the Arab world. . . .The atom bomb will be something that Saddam Hussein desperately needs now."[14] These sentiments were underscored by U.S. nuclear expert Paul Leventhal, who described Saddam Hussein's persistent desire to acquire nuclear weapons as follows, "[Saddam Hussein wants nuclear bombs]. . . because it's his way to match Israel. Also, these are accepted weapons in the international community. Not only are they accepted weapons, but they are also weapons that bring maximum prestige. Nuclear gives him status in the region that will totally eclipse any other Arab state."[15]

Khidhir Hamza stresses that you need only look at the numbers to comprehend the importance of nuclear might to Saddam Hussein. According to the former nuclear development specialist for Iraq, Saddam Hussein has only several hundred people working on biological and chemical weapons while 12,000 are actively engaged in nuclear weapons work. Approximately 5,000 of these were supposedly added after the Gulf War while UNSCOM inspectors went about their business.

Yet even before the Gulf War, Iraq had come dangerously close to having nuclear weapons. Looking back, U.S. officials now acknowledge that prior to the Gulf War they had seriously underestimated Saddam Hussein's nuclear weapons program. Supposedly, the CIA thought that Iraq was about a decade away from perfecting a nuclear bomb but that was largely because the International Atomic Energy Agency (IAEA) entirely misjudged Iraq's nuclear capabilities early on.

Although inspections, greater overall enhanced scrutiny, and the U.S. air raids have somewhat lessened Iraq's nuclear potential, some nuclear scientists believe Saddam Hussein could catch up a lot faster than most people would like to believe. "A bomb is an intellectual product," noted nuclear weapons expert Gary Milhollin. "The main thing you need is knowledge, and Iraq has that. They developed it before the war. They've been working on it since the war. And that knowledge can be converted into things very quickly."[16]

Keeping this knowledge precisely where he wants it has not always been easy for Saddam Hussein. As might be expected, the Iraqi dictator was not pleased with the number of high-level defectors from the ranks and has long relied on heavy-handed coercion to force nuclear scientists and technicians to keep Iraq's nuclear program on track.

Saddam Hussein has repeatedly demonstrated that he'll use bribery to elicit cooperation from his nuclear workforce and if that doesn't work, he is not skittish about resorting to torture. The brutal tactics begin with depriving the victim of food and water for a few days. "Then they start beating him up," Hamza explained in further describing Saddam's operating methods. "They hang him [the victim] up by a hand or a foot for quite a period until he starts really breaking down."[17]

Besides the local talent pressed into service, Saddam Hussein has also gone to great lengths to cultivate a substantial international network of outside assistance to achieve his nuclear goals. This includes a string of front companies and smugglers whose sole purpose is to supply parts and materials for illegal weapons. Hussein also gained access to ready-made vital components designed according to his needs and specifications. Among these are devices to trigger nuclear reactions in missile warheads.

In describing the Iraqi leader's attempts to have some of the more sensitive aspects of his nuclear weapons development done outside of the country, Khidhir Hamza said, "The idea is to do it outside and then bring the thing back home. . . . There are hundreds of these companies in Jordan. They have a whole system of runners in ordinary cars."[18] Numerous other available front companies are scattered about the area as well.

The illicit parts and materials are smuggled into the country in a variety of ways. Small but valuable components are frequently disguised and hidden in personal luggage while some larger items are wrapped in plastic and placed in the empty tanks of oil trucks returning to Iraq. Weapons parts in foam-padded bags have been brought across borders by bribing a guard with just a bottle of whiskey or a few dollars. A substantial amount of materials including numerous larger items are smuggled through Turkey, where border controls are the least stringent.

Once inside Iraq the contraband items are shipped to well-disguised nuclear weapons centers guarded by Saddam Hussein's most trusted security forces. There nuclear experts integrate the necessary items into the existing weapon's framework. As nuclear expert Anthony H. Cordesman described how the imported material is processed, "It's scattered throughout the country. Not only do you have small centers and duplicative efforts, but you have groups that are now dedicated to using civilian covers to hide and maneuver what they have left around."[19] By placing these essential items in civilian strongholds, Hussein hoped to hide his efforts from both the watchful gaze of U.N. inspectors and U.S.-British air attacks.

Hussein is also believed to have hidden bank accounts from the Persian Gulf to Latin America to finance these endeavors. In many cases the Iraqi government sent relatives of officials, trusted businessmen, and even phony defectors to open bank accounts abroad. At times small businesses were also set up to launder potential dollars earmarked for weaponry smuggling and nuclear research. In all these situations the front runners knew that their family and friends were still in Iraq and would not be safe unless they performed as expected.

In addition, governments friendly to Iraq such as Yemen, Sudan, and Libya have been of assistance with Hussein's offshore research needs or even in allowing him to set up small parts production centers. During the late 1990s U.S. nuclear experts learned that the director general of Iraq's nuclear research center, Abdulkadir Rahman, had been visiting India's leading nuclear research laboratory. These trips would have remained secret if a computer hacker had not broken into the Indian center's files. Khidhir Hamza confirmed that at one time Iraq had developed a "deep and multilayered cooperation" with India. The relationship had cooled for a time but Hamza added that "it seems to be back now."[20]

There's also proof that Iraq sent officials to Russia to purchase nuclear materials, delivery system parts, and technology. While it's rumored that many Russian scientists have found work in Iraq, the numbers may actually be much smaller than believed. That's because Saddam Hussein likes to have complete control over his workers and this might not be possible with foreign scientists. Spurgeon Keany, a former U.S. government arms official who is now president of the Arms Control Association in Washington, D.C., pointed out that while Iraqi nuclear scientists often function in a state of fear, nuclear scientists from other countries would be able to leave at will—this would be especially true of those whose families were not with them. Keany further noted that if U.N. inspections were to resume in Iraq, foreign scientists would be more likely to stand out, drawing the attention of inspectors and reporters.

While UNSCOM inspectors were still in Iraq, they were keenly aware that many of the key elements they were looking for were likely to be found in other countries and that this required special vigilance on their part. "Offshore work is more difficult to investigate," UNSCOM inspector Charles Duelfer confirmed. "We have seen what happened in the past. Iraq set up front companies in the 1980s and it's reasonable to expect a continuation. We have to monitor this very carefully."[21] With UNSCOM out of Iraq now it's expected that Saddam Hussein's efforts along these lines will become increasingly blatant.

It's impossible to predict just what will happen in the future, although most U.S. policy makers agree that Saddam Hussein will probably continue to try to build a nuclear arsenal. Meanwhile, many world leaders would prefer to keep nuclear weaponry out of the Iraqi president's reach. U.S. policy makers further feel the need to guard against possible retribution, nuclear or otherwise, for the air attacks on Iraq. This could take the form of either a military attack or a terrorist attack and could possibly occur even years afterward.

"People underestimate memories in the Arab world," former Commander Peay predicted. "And this is a guy with tremendous hatred for us and for the Kuwaitis. Now we've embarrassed him. He's hunkered down but he won't forget. And now the problem is policy. I don't think our Arab allies like this to go on all the time. I don't think we can keep bombing [Iraq] year after year. What do we do next? That's where we're caught."[22]

Obviously there isn't a simple solution in dealing with Iraq, and sadly nuclear development in the Middle East doesn't stop at its borders. Iran, the largest and most heavily populated country in the area, is proud of its long and distinguished history and believes it should be a regional power with nuclear capability. To that end it has begun to develop nuclear weapons along with an array of missile delivery systems capable of reaching countries as far away as the United States.

Iran's relationship with the United States over the years has been far from ideal. During the 1960s and 1970s the United States supported the shah of Iran, who sought to westernize his country. The shah's policies were opposed by many of his people, especially the Islamic clergy. The shah was deposed in 1979 by the Ayatollah Khomeini, who established Iran's current Islamic republic. According to Peter Tarnoff, undersecretary for political affairs, "We know that Iran harbors a deep resentment about America's relationship with the shah. Today, Tehran [Iran's capital] fears America's military prowess in the Gulf and objects to our prominent regional influence."[23]

Iran has also had an uneasy relationship with some of its Arab neighbors. In the 1980s it endured an eight-year war with Iraq. In addition, Iran assumes a hostile posture toward the Jewish state of Israel, which is already a nuclear power. Therefore, if Iran were to acquire nuclear weapons there are a number of potential situations in which they might eventually be put to use.

In defense of its nuclear program, Iran has argued that it needs to develop nuclear energy to generate electric power, but defense experts doubt that this is the only reason. In any case, that explanation does not account for the time, effort, and financial resources Iran has poured into its missile delivery program. Such land, sea, and air delivery systems mated with a nuclear warhead are crucial to a successful offensive assault. They are the other half of the nuclear equation.

Through satellite photographs, Western intelligence sources have learned that Iran has successfully tested powerful liquid-fueled missile engines. For some time there's been an Iran-Russia connection in developing both long- and short-range missiles capable of carrying nuclear warheads. Initially Iran purchased its rocket engines from North Korea but these outdated models were upgraded by Russian engineers and technicians from a Russian weapons facility. Iran's latest missile design is partly based on the Soviet SS-4 strategic rocket developed during the Cold War.

Russian scientists began actively working on Iran's long-range missile development in 1994. There's evidence to suggest that's when Russian technicians began visiting the country's Defense Technology and Science Research Center, a top secret facility about 50 miles (80 kilometers) from Iran's capital. Since that time Russian technicians have worked at a number of Iranian missile centers, including factory and design sites throughout the country. "After that, Iran's missile program jelled," notes Patrick Clawson, an analyst at the National Defense University in Washington, D.C.[24]

With the Russians' aid, Iran has almost perfected two types of missiles. The Shahab-3, which should be ready in the near future, has a reach of over 800 miles (1,290 kilometers), allowing it to hit every major urban center in Israel as well as bases in Saudi Arabia and Turkey where U.S. military forces are presently stationed. The second more powerful missile being built is the Shahab-4, which will be able to deliver a one ton warhead 1,250 miles (2,000 kilometers). Some of Iran's solid-fuel missiles in the design stage could travel distances of 2,800 miles (4,500 kilometers) to reach European cities and there are plans for a 6,300-mile (10,100-kilometer) missile that could strike areas on the East Coast of the United States.

Intelligence sources have revealed that Russian scientists and technicians still regularly travel to Iran to provide technical expertise on missile development. However, Russian officials deny helping Iran with its missile program. Transferring the technology from its SS-4 rockets to delivery systems for Iran would violate the 1995 Missile Technology Control Regime signed by the Russian government. Revamping the SS-4 rockets for Iranian use further shows complete disregard for the 1987 Intermediate-Range Nuclear Forces Treaty. Under this agreement, signed by both the former Soviet Union and the United States, Russia agreed to destroy all its SS-4 missiles along with other similar ones. Despite increasing evidence to the contrary, high-ranking Russian officials continue to deny their country's involvement. "While we appreciate such assurances," State Department official Robert Einhorn commented, "we remain disturbed by the discrepancy between them and what reportedly is occurring."[25]

In response, the United States has taken steps to try to contain Iran's nuclear weapons and missile buildup. U.S. officials have worked with other governments on instituting export controls to prevent Iran from obtaining sensitive dual-use items and technology that could be used for military purposes. President Clinton also imposed an embargo against Iran. All trade and investment with this Middle Eastern nation was cut off and other nations were encouraged to do the same.

The idea behind the embargo was to lessen Iran's financial resources, thereby hindering its ability to finance nuclear weapons projects. By making Iran pay a high price for its unacceptable activities, the United States hopes to convince Iranian leaders that it's in their country's best interest to abandon these policies.

In addition, the United States has provided aid to its ally Israel to help develop its ARROW antimissile program. Ideally, Israel would have this defense system solidly in place by the time Iran perfects its missile systems. The United States has also taken steps so that other allies in the region could defend themselves against a nuclear missile attack from Iran or Iraq as well. Through a "shared early warning system," countries such as Kuwait, Saudi Arabia, Bahrain, the United Arab Emirates, Oman, and Qatar would be hooked up to U.S. intelligence satellites that can immediately detect missiles launched from Iran or Iraq through infrared sensors. "We would [ideally] do this with all the [friendly] Gulf states to have a direct link between what our sensors are able to pick up and to communicate that to the Gulf," Secretary of Defense William Cohen stated.[26]

An information exchange of this nature would be valuable to U.S. Gulf allies since both Iran and Iraq are developing missiles that could easily reach all the Gulf states. While there appears to be no immediate danger, at times various pressures in the region have generated tensions that could result in a future attack.

Besides alerting these nations to a missile assault, the system would also benefit the United States military, as there are thousands of U.S. forces stationed in the area. So far the Gulf states have been ambivalent about accepting the offer. Having already been criticized by Islamic factions for being too helpful to the U.S. military, they are concerned about their image. Yet, they are concerned enough about the missile buildup in Iran and Iraq not to have said no yet either.

Libya's another country in the area that has tried to obtain nuclear weapons for decades. As early as 1970, Libyan leader Colonel Muammar Kaddafi approached China hoping to purchase nuclear weaponry, but was rebuffed. Over the years Libya has spent quite a bit of money setting up nuclear research facilities. However, even after obtaining substantial assistance from the former Soviet Union, the country never came close to successfully producing a nuclear bomb.

Nevertheless in the 1990s there were new reports indicating that Libya had not given up its dream of becoming a

*Libyan president Muammar Kaddafi, shown here addressing a cheering crowd of Palestinians, is a strong advocate of nuclear capability for the Arab countries, a stance he feels is justified by the world's unconfirmed suspicions that nearby Israel is a nuclear power.*

nuclear power. In March 1996 then CIA director John M. Deutch said that Kaddafi was "trying to recruit [local] scientists in developing nuclear weapons, although it is doubtful that Tripoli [Libya's capital] could produce a nuclear weapon without significant foreign technical assistance."[27] U.S. officials don't doubt that if weapons-grade nuclear material was made available on the international black market, Libya would be a likely buyer.

For some time Colonel Muammar Kaddafi had insisted that Arab states should manufacture nuclear weapons to counter Israel's nuclear might. In January 1996, Libya's official news agency reiterated Kaddafi's position stating, "The Arabs who are threatened by the Israeli nuclear weapons have the right to try in any way possible to possess these weapons so that a balance is achieved, and so that the region is not left at the mercy of the Israelis."[28]

Although the Israeli government has never openly admitted having a nuclear arsenal, its existence is not a secret. Israel refrained from using nuclear weapons even when attacked by Arab nations in both 1967 and 1973 and faced with the very real possibility of defeat. Instead, Israel has relied on the deterrent value of its nuclear bombs—making certain that if an enemy attacked it using unconventional weapons (nuclear, chemical, or biological) that country would have to consider Israel's potential nuclear retaliation.

Nevertheless, the rapid escalation of nuclear capability in the Middle East is disturbing. So far Israel has demonstrated restraint with regard to its nuclear arsenal but if Iraq, Iran, and Libya achieve nuclear status, could they be counted on to do the same? Furthermore, if any of these Arab nations launch a nuclear strike against Israel, it's likely that the Jewish state will respond similarly. In a region where tremendous tensions exist and military confrontations are common, the stakes are growing increasingly high.

It came as a shock on a pleasant May morning in 1998. U.S. satellite photos and intelligence sources had not predicted a nuclear blast in South Asia, but at a little after 6:00 A.M. seismograph needles on instruments in a number of countries registered a tremendous rumble in the ground that could only mean one thing–there had been a nuclear explosion. India later claimed that not one but three bombs were detonated, equaling about double the explosive force of the bomb dropped on Hiroshima during World War II. The nuclear surprises weren't over; two days later another two bombs were exploded. It wasn't war–instead India was testing its new nuclear devices in the Pokharan desert.

The unexpected detonations resulted in a great deal of criticism heaped on America's intelligence-gathering services. "I am astonished that India was able to catch the U.S. intelligence capability sound asleep at the switch," Senate Foreign Relations Committee chairman Jesse Helms openly commented.[1] Some insisted that if President Clinton had known about India's nuclear test plans in advance, he might have been able to stop it and possibly forestall what could turn into a regional weapons escalation.

White House critics claimed that the administration spent so much time trying to prevent a nuclear buildup in "outlaw," or "rogue," nations like Iran, Iraq, and Libya that equally serious threats posed by other countries were ignored. Undeniably, India and Pakistan have now acquired nuclear arsenals that threaten regional and international security. But could President Clinton have done anything to stop the nuclear testing and arms buildup?

In the past India has refused to sign the 1968 Nuclear Nonproliferation Treaty (NPT)–an agreement through which nonnuclear countries promise not to develop nuclear weapons. It also failed to sign the 1996 Comprehensive Test-Ban Treaty, which prohibits nuclear testing. When pressured to do so, India frequently argued that the treaties would only be fair if the large nuclear nations took tangible steps to totally destroy their arsenals.

Yet in 1998, Russia still had a total of 10,240 operational nuclear warheads while China had 400; France, 450; Britain, 260; and Israel between 70 and 125. The United States had 8,420 actual nuclear warheads with an additional 12,000 in reserve and/or awaiting dismantlement. The Nuclear Nonproliferation Treaty provides that the five major nuclear powers will reduce and eventually disarm their nuclear arsenals, but as of yet none of these countries has a published timetable documenting when all their nuclear weapons will be destroyed. In fact the United States, Russia, Great Britain, and France have even insisted on retaining some nuclear weapons for deterrence. It's also been argued that while the United States no longer actually tests nuclear weapons, it violates the spirit of the Comprehensive Test-Ban Treaty by conducting computer simulation and subcritical tests that provide the same data.

India feels that the existence of nuclear weapons drastically alters the nature of national security everywhere. Indian leaders agree that the world would be safer if there were no nuclear weapons. But they believe that the security interests of all nations are equally legitimate and that gives India the right to have nuclear weapons for its own protection.

While President Clinton described India's nuclear test imperative as a "fundamental mistake," India's prime minister Atal Bihari Vajpayee staunchly defended his country's position. When asked why the tests were conducted, he replied,"We did so on the basis of our own careful appraisal of the regional- and global-security scenario. Every nation has the sovereign right to address its national security needs in an appropriate manner consistent with the imperative to preserve regional and global peace. We have exercised this right."[2]

Looking at India's geographical position and its relations with its neighbors, it's clear that Indians do not enjoy the same sense of security that people in the United States do. To its northeast lies China, a nuclear power and military giant that in 1962 successfully invaded India. The Indians have never forgotten their stinging defeat and are keenly aware that presently their army is only about a third as large as China's and their air force just a quarter the size of their hostile neighbor's.

On another of India's borders lies Pakistan, a Muslim state with which the largely Hindu nation of India has been at war three times since 1947. Most recently tensions have arisen between India and Pakistan over the control of Kash-

WE PROUD ON OUR NUCLEAR TEST

Despite the English-language error on their sign, the message of these Indian women comes through loud and clear. They are proud, indeed ecstatic, over their nation's newly-developed nuclear ability—a stance shared by their prime minister, Atal Bihari Vajpayee.

mir, a mostly Muslim region situated at the northern end of the India-Pakistan border.

Currently the territory is divided between the two countries along a 500-mile (800-kilometer) Line of Control. However, there's hardly been political calm in this picturesque region. Various militant groups–some wanting Indian control, others wanting Pakistani rule, and still others desiring an independent Kashmir–have risen up and fought one another as well as the authorities. So far the fighting has resulted in the loss of over 30,000 lives and created many more refugees.

The conflict between India and Pakistan over Kashmir predates the acquisition of nuclear weapons by either country and actually extends back to 1947, when India and Pakistan gained their independence from British rule. Despite the fact that Kashmir has a largely Muslim population, its Hindu monarch chose to join India. Pakistan was outraged by the decision. Seeing itself as the Muslim homeland in South Asia, it insisted that Kashmir be incorporated into Pakistan.

Pakistan requested that the people of Kashmir be allowed to vote on which country they wanted to be part of– a solution that was adopted as a United Nations resolution. But so far Indian leaders have not agreed to this. Meanwhile there appears to be no end to the dispute, which at times nearly takes on the fervor of a holy war. Pakistani militants have shot at the Indians on the other side of the Line of Control and the Indians fire back.

Some in the international community hoped that with India and Pakistan each aware that the other has nuclear weapons, both might take a step back and think about what further escalation in Kashmir could eventually lead to. However, this hasn't happened and as the violence continues, the situation begs for some type of resolution. As Mushadhid Husain, the Pakistani government's minister of information, suggested, "Let us focus on resolving Kashmir, because now . . . there is an inextricable linkage between Kashmir and the larger issue of peace, stability, and security in South Asia."[3] Yet the fierce rivalry and troubled history between India and Pakistan makes any type of negotiation difficult.

As required by U.S. law, President Clinton ordered economic sanctions against India following its recent round of nuclear tests. All aid except funds for food and humanitarian concerns was discontinued, as was Overseas Private Investment Corporation financing for the U.S. firms doing business in India. India also lost millions in export credits and military aid. In addition, the sanctions meant an end to U.S. bank loans, and President Clinton pledged to oppose loans to India from international institutions. Japan, India's most significant benefactor, followed the lead of the United States, stopping millions in economic aid as well. Denmark put $28 million slated for India on hold while Germany did the same with $160 million in development aid.

If the Indian government's actions were condemned in the international community, the response certainly differed at home. Indian prime minister Atal Bihari Vajpayee proudly boasted to his public, "India is now a nuclear weapons state. We have the capacity for a big bomb now."[4] His enthusiasm was shared by the cheering crowds that gathered outside his home, shouted his name, and threw red rose petals at his feet.

Most newspapers throughout the country reflected the nation's exhilaration, reporting India's new nuclear status in glowing terms. "As an Indian, I am proud it was done in

India by Indians," said Tushar Gandhi, great-grandson of Mahatma, the famous Indian leader and advocate of non-violence.[5] "It had to be done," further underscored Balasaheb Thackeray, leader of Shiu Seng, an Indian right wing party.[6] A public opinion poll taken shortly after the nuclear tests indicated that 91 percent of the Indian people heartily supported their government's actions.

Aware of the tension between Pakistan and India, Washington feared that Pakistan would initiate its own round of nuclear tests to match India's prowess. Both an array of U.S. officials and President Clinton himself tried to talk Pakistani leaders out of responding in kind to the developments in India. In his fourth call to Pakistani prime minister Nawaz Sharif in a two-week period, the U.S. president urged him not to proceed with nuclear testing. "This is a trap India wants to lure you into," Clinton warned. "India would welcome testing because it will diffuse the pressure on them."[7]

Sharif acknowledged Clinton's point but declared that by then "the matter was out of [his] hands."[8] There were those in Pakistan who felt that India had forced them to match its nuclear test efforts. Ignoring it, the Pakistanis believed, would be seen as recognizing India's regional dominance and superiority. That was one road Pakistan was not willing to take. "If we don't test we lose the credibility of our so-called nuclear capability," said Shireen Mazari, a respected Pakistani military analyst. "It means gradual Indian dominance over the region, which we can't accept. It's a question of when [to conduct nuclear testing] not if."[9]

Just weeks after India's tests, Pakistan detonated five nuclear bombs of their own. Like the Indians, the Pakistanis were jubilant over their successful nuclear tests, and following the exercise Prime Minister Nawaz Sharif proudly proclaimed, "Today we have settled the score with India."[10]

Pakistan's dream of being a nuclear power isn't new. Following India's first nuclear blast in 1974, former Pakistani president Zulfikar Ali Bhutto repeatedly declared that if necessary Pakistanis would "eat grass" so that the nation's resources could be used for nuclear development. Even after being deposed by a military dictator while awaiting execution in prison, Bhutto spoke glowingly of the nuclear system he started and his dream of building an "Islamic bomb." In 1978, Bhutto wrote that while Christian, Jewish, and Hindu civilizations had nuclear weapons "Islamic civilization" did not. Yet he and his followers ardently hoped that the situation was about to change.

Bhutto's daughter Benazir shares her father's enthusiasm for developing an Islamic nuclear arsenal. Benazir, who was educated at Harvard University and also formerly served as Pakistan's prime minister, now heads the opposition party in Pakistan. After India's May 1998 round of nuclear tests, she urged Pakistan's citizens not to allow their nation to become a second-rate power in the region and accused her rival, Prime Minister Sharif, of "not having the guts to detonate a nuclear bomb."[11] If Sharif had any inkling of playing down the competition with India, Benazir's actions made it even more difficult for him to do so.

Pakistan's reciprocal nuclear tests were not a surprise to Washington, only a disappointment. "I cannot believe," President Clinton said, "that we are about to start off the twenty-first century by having the Indian Subcontinent repeat the worst mistakes of the twentieth century."[12] Undoubtedly many felt that the "tit for tat" nature of the new arms race in South Asia was hauntingly similar to the Cold

*Pakistani prime minister Nawaz Sharif (left) answers a question about the disputed Kashmir region while his Indian counterpart, Atal Bihari Vajpayee, seems to glower beside him. This February 1999 meeting, the first between the two arch rivals since each had flexed his nuclear muscle, seemed to have positive overtones as each pledged to take immediate steps to reduce the risk of nuclear conflict and to intensify efforts to work out disputes at the bargaining table.*

War between the United States and the former Soviet Union. Yet while there are vivid parallels between the two situations, there are important differences as well.

For one thing, the United States and the Soviet Union never shared a common border as India and Pakistan do. The distrust and ill will between the two nations was not fueled by religious passions such as the Hindu-Muslim conflict in South Asia and therefore remained less emotionally charged. The thought of religious fervor overtaking the cool analytical thinking needed for nuclear deterrence is more than a little unsettling to many.

In addition, both Pakistan and India lack the technological safeguards that protected the system during the Cold War from sabotage or the accidental detonation of a bomb. Neither country has a satellite detection system, adequate monitoring devices, or double launch codes. When India as well as Pakistan tested its missile delivery systems, each had no notion of what the other had done. "Neither side has the least idea what the other is deploying," a U.S. Pentagon official said in sizing up the situation. "In a crisis, they would have to assume the worst."[13]

U.S. studies on the effects of a double nuclear strike between India and Pakistan are terrifying. Estimates show that within the first few hours over 17 million Pakistanis and 29 million Indians would be killed. Medical assistance would be largely unavailable to the injured, as Pakistan has only forty-seven doctors per thousand people and India has just forty-eight per thousand.

A 1992 U.S. Air Force study indicated that about 100 million people could eventually perish from the blasts' effects and that much of South Asia would remain coated with nuclear fallout for years to come. Yet following its round of nuclear tests, Pakistan's prime minister declared, "Today the flames of the nuclear fire are all over. And I am thankful to God that we have jumped into these flames . . . with courage."[14]

While comprehensive safeguards against nuclear disaster have not yet worked out in South Asia, both Pakistan and India have actively focused on securing delivery systems to make certain that their bombs reach their intended targets. After all, developing a nuclear weapon isn't very useful if your enemy knows you can't send it to his backyard. To that end, India and Pakistan have both worked on a variety of missiles capable of delivering nuclear warheads.

Prior to the May 1998 nuclear tests, Western nations mistakenly thought that India and Pakistan had poured so much of their resources into building nuclear bombs that their delivery systems lagged somewhat behind. But in reality this was hardly the case.

With the help of India's enemy China, Pakistan adapted the short-range Chinese M-11 missile to meet its needs early on. But since these would not reach sufficiently far into the heart of India, it set about acquiring long-range delivery systems. Pakistan's long-range missile is called the Ghauri– not coincidentally named after a twelfth-century Muslim raider who overthrew a Hindu leader. The Ghauri was based on a North Korean missile known as the No Dong, which in turn had been based on an old Soviet scud missile. Intelligence sources believe that the North Koreans supplied Pakistan with blueprints, answers to technical questions, and a few sample missiles to study.

The Chinese were also helpful in revamping the No Dong missile. They assisted Pakistani scientists in improving the missile's precision as well as in enhancing other aspects of its delivery performance. Pakistan claims that the Ghauri missile was built in response to India's arms escalation and the placement of Indian missiles close to the Indian-Pakistan border.

The Pakistanis were also made uncomfortable by the remarks of India's home minister L. K. Advani, the former president of the Hindu nationalist Bharatiya Janata Party (BJP), when shortly after his nation's nuclear tests, he announced, "Islamabad [Pakistan's capital] should realize the change in the geostrategic situation in the region and roll back its anti-India policy, especially with regard to Kashmir."[15]

In response the Pakistanis announced that their new long-range Ghauri missiles are in the process of being outfitted with nuclear warheads. However, later on A. O. Khan, head of Pakistan's nuclear and missile program, admitted they were only ". . . ready to build nuclear-tipped Ghauri missiles if the government gives the order."[16] Nevertheless few in the international community felt relieved.

That's because India, like Pakistan, has been actively upgrading its weapons delivery systems. Intelligence sources revealed that in addition to its land-based missiles, it's currently working on a two-pronged approach to develop both cruise and sea-launched ballistic missiles along with a nuclear-powered submarine from which to deploy them. With the help of Russian expertise and technology, Indian scientists will be able to complete a submarine-launched nuclear weapons system that could reach China, crippling some of its major cities. The Indians hope the threat of nuclear retaliation would prevent China from ever invading their country again as well as somewhat evening the balance of power between the two nations.

Many international onlookers are as concerned about the delivery systems as they are about the actual bombs developed. "Both sides [India and Pakistan] are working on longer-range missiles, and that is worrisome," said Pentagon spokesman Kenneth Bacon. "It's part of the pattern of proliferation that we think is destabilizing to the people on the Indian subcontinent, and it does increase the risk of miscalculation or overstepping."[17]

A further threat to the United States and its allies is that India's nuclear buildup will spur China on to build additional missiles. China ceased its nuclear testing program in 1996 in response to overwhelming pressure from the international community. But could the Chinese once again feel the need to rekindle it?

Intelligence sources already indicate that China is taking steps to upgrade its military. Ironically, there's evidence that some of the high-tech measures being instituted were acquired either through spying or outright purchases from U.S. military surplus sales. "The Chinese will use anybody who's available or has access," a CIA source said. "It's across the board."[18] In recent years as relations between China and the United States thawed somewhat, Chinese scientists also gained more access to U.S. military operations and it's been alleged that Chinese researchers visiting U.S. nuclear weapons labs in the 1980s and 1990s pilfered design information for their bombs and nuclear warheads.

In one incident Taiwan-born scientist Wen Ho Lee was fired from Los Alamos National Laboratory for disclosing sensitive nuclear data to China. The scientist was at the center of a U.S. intelligence investigation in which it's believed secret information was given to the Chinese that enabled them to develop miniaturized warheads. These warheads can be launched from a single missile at multiple targets. Previously, China's nuclear weapons had been about a generation behind those of the United States.

In an unrelated incident in 1999, federal agents in California arrested Chinese citizen Yao Yi and charged him with attempting to obtain items vital to missile guidance systems. Yao had tried to purchase fiber-optic gyroscopes from a Massachusetts defense contractor but the U.S. State Department refused to approve the transaction since China is a "prohibited destination" for gyroscopes. Determined to secure them anyway, Yao then attempted to buy the gyroscopes from another company that assured him it would get the merchandise to China. Yao had no way of knowing that the company was actually a front for a sting operation set up by the U.S. Customs Service.

Yao Yi later insisted that the gyroscopes were not intended for military purposes but were to be used for a high-speed train navigation project. Although gyroscopes can be used in railroad work, federal authorities doubt Yao's claims since the associate he worked with had been simultaneously trying to purchase the infrared sensors used in missiles. One federal agent also said that using this type of gyroscope for high-speed train navigation "would be like flying an F-14 to the grocery store."[19]

Unfortunately, U.S. companies may have inadvertently helped the Chinese improve its ballistic missile capability. Since President Reagan's administration, the United States has been using Chinese rockets to put its satellites into space. They were inexpensive and filled a gap in the U.S. space launch industry's supplies. However, some in government had reservations about the arrangement, believing that the relationship allowed China to gain valuable information to improve its long-range missiles. This included data to better predict the effects of wind shear and other forces on rocket flight. When asked about who profits most from the joint U.S.-China satellite ventures, an Air Force official indicated that there was little doubt on this matter. He readily admitted, "Definitely, the Chinese get more."[20]

Most recently there have been inquiries into whether some U.S. companies working with China might have revealed sensitive information which could violate "national security concerns." The United States has no desire to help China improve its ballistic missile capacity since Chinese missiles can be used to carry nuclear warheads as well as space satellites.

A summary of China's access to classified nuclear information can be found in a 1999 congressional committee document known as the Cox report. According to this scathing account, the Chinese pilfered valuable nuclear weapons data from U.S. laboratories as well as were assisted in their research and development efforts by various U.S. companies.

The report claims that these corporations helped the Chinese through "transferred missile design information and know-how . . . without obtaining legally required licenses." It further alleges that stolen design "information has improved the reliability of [China's] rockets [which are] useful for [both] civilian and military purposes." Perhaps the document's most disturbing charge was that the Chinese had secured sensitive data on every existing U.S. nuclear warhead.

Though the Cox report is chilling, some have argued that in many instances it presents the worst possible scenarios as well as overemphasizes some facts. "There are, unfortunately, a number of places where the report reaches to make a point," South Carolina Representative John Spratt noted, "and, frankly, exaggerates."[21]

There's also been some discussion of the validity and relevance of some of the report's assertions. In one case, the information came from a double agent who voluntarily turned over the materials to the CIA. This caused officials to wonder if the Chinese had purposely planted it for them to see. But even if the effects of China's efforts were less damaging than the report indicates, classified information still fell into the wrong hands.

This also raises a further concern. It's known that for some time China has actively marketed and sold whole missiles as well as smaller missile parts to a number of countries. These include nations that it would not be in the best interest of the United States to assist. As one Senate aide described the situation, "We haven't just helped China. We've helped all of China's customers too."[22]

China is presently constructing twenty new Donfeng-31 intercontinental ballistic missiles with a 5,000-mile (8,000-kilometer) range that could send a nuclear warhead to the U.S. West Coast. However, at this time defense experts doubt that China's military buildup presents any real threat to the United States. Instead, it's far more likely that the Chinese want to remain the dominant power in Asia. "China isn't trying to project power to San Francisco Bay," explained Ralph Cossa, head of the Pacific Coast Forum Center for Strategic and International Studies. "It's trying to project power to the South China Sea."[23] But that's a goal Indian officials don't feel bodes well for their country.

Following its May 1998 nuclear tests, President Clinton imposed the same economic sanctions on Pakistan as he did on India. Prior to the tests, Pakistani prime minister Sharif knew that sanctions would be extremely hard on his country as its economy is heavily dependent on foreign aid. Yet after the nuclear trials he said that he never considered taking "all the gifts and compensation that were being offered to us" to refrain from nuclear testing. Sharif warned his people that the sanctions would mean that "difficulties and hard times will increase" and also told them "you will have to be patient, courageous." He further announced to the world that Pakistanis "are ready to die for their honor."[24]

At first many wondered if the sanctions would truly make a significant difference. India would feel less of an impact since its economy is stronger than Pakistan's and, in addition, many other countries, including some European nations, refused to impose their own sanctions on these South Asian states. "I don't think the sanctions are going to change a . . . thing," remarked Scott Thompson, director of International Development Studies at Tufts University. "It's a race to the scaffold now. . . . There is a nuclear arms race in South Asia. The real danger of nuclear weapons being used somewhere in the world is here, and now we've moved from a 10 to 20 percent possibility to a 30 to 40 percent possibility."[25]

However, as it turned out, the economic sanctions did have an effect and since they were imposed, U.S. officials have been actively working with both India and Pakistan to end their nuclear weapons escalation. The United States wants India to sign the test-ban treaty and stop manufacturing parts and materials for nuclear weapons. U.S. officials are also insisting that the development of nuclear-tipped missiles be held to a minimum. The Indian government, on the other hand, wants all the economic sanctions lifted and the freedom to build what they've referred to as a "credible nuclear deterrent."

In accordance with U.S. demands, leaders from India and Pakistan talked in a series of formal meetings about issues mutually affecting their nations. Though not a great deal of progress was made, President Clinton lifted some of the sanctions on both nations to reward them for their beginning efforts. To India's chagrin, Pakistan was relieved of more sanctions due to its severely unstable economy. The United States feared the situation might become desperate there unless the World Bank resumed lending to Pakistan. As one U.S. official put it, "There is nothing more dangerous than a bankrupt country trying to raise money—with nothing to sell but an atom bomb."[26]

Pramod Mahajan, a Hindu nationalist who serves in India's Parliament, made no secret of his disgust at what he saw as blatantly unfair treatment. "If you made a law," he said, "that you would hang someone for murder and then you say, 'I won't hang him because he's thin, but I'll hang him because he's strong,' what kind of law is that? A murder is a murder."[27]

U.S. officials felt it was the best solution for a difficult situation but hoped it would not impede the continuing dialogue between India and the United States or India and Pakistan. There was something of a breakthrough in February 1999, when Atal Behari Vajpayee took a historic weekend trip to Pakistan, making him the first Indian prime minister to visit the country in a decade. There the two new nuclear powers worked out some of their differences in two signed documents and a short statement. "We must bring peace to our people," Pakistani prime minister Nawaz Sharif said at a joint news conference following the signing. "We must bring posterity to our people. We owe this to ourselves and to future generations."[28]

Although the United States along with other countries had hoped for a dramatic conclusion, the agreements arrived at have been described as somewhat "long on good intentions and short on details."[29] Nevertheless, India and Pakistan have now at least promised to alert one another to "any accidental, unauthorized or unexplained incident" that could inadvertently trigger a nuclear disaster.[30]

The danger of instability in nuclear-capable nations was underscored in October 1999 when a sudden military coup in Pakistan ousted Prime Minister Nawaz Sharif.

The United States would like to see peace and stability in South Asia but there are limits to what it can do to achieve this. As Michael McCurry, former White House spokesperson, put it, "The United States of America, despite all its wealth and its might, cannot control every event, every place in the world—particularly in a place where for five decades now governments have fought wars and people have lived with incredible tension."[31]

# 5
## NORTH KOREA

Ascertaining North Korea's precise nuclear status has always been difficult. That's because even though the country signed the Nuclear Nonproliferation Treaty in 1985, it has violated the agreement in a number of ways. These include not permitting the IAEA to conduct special inspections in 1992 at several key facilities at the Yongbyon Nuclear Research Center, including that of an operational experimental nuclear power reactor, a partially finished large-scale plutonium reprocessing plant, several plutonium extraction facilities, a testing area, and a partly completed nuclear power reactor.

Nevertheless, by the early 1990s, U.S. intelligence learned that North Korea had extracted as much as 12 kilograms of plutonium—enough to produce one or two nuclear bombs. And in May 1994 it was further revealed that, if reprocessed, the North Koreans would by then have had sufficient plutonium for four or five bombs.

In response, the United States began a series of high-level talks with North Korean leaders to try to work out a solution. The result was the October 1994 U.S.-North Korean "Agreed Framework" under which North Korea agreed to immediately freeze its nuclear program and then proceed to dismantle its nuclear facilities, which would have permitted North Korea to manufacture numerous nuclear weapons annually. Among other concessions, North Korea agreed to allow the International Atomic Energy Agency to inspect two of its undeclared nuclear waste sites, which would provide the agency with more information on its past plutonium production.

In return for the halt in plutonium production, a group of countries led by the United States and South Korea agreed to give North Korea fuel oil and to build two replacement power reactors in which the spent fuel generated cannot easily be converted into bombs. The United States regarded the agreement as a diplomatic triumph and assured the public that in lacking plutonium, North Korea's military nuclear goals would be a thing of the past.

Despite Washington's boasts of having "frozen and stopped" North Korea's efforts to establish a nuclear arsenal, new information from reliable intelligence sources indicated that this might not be so. The country may still be carrying on an active nuclear weapons program. Much of the work may be carried on in secret sites in the North Korean countryside. Spy-satellite photos of the region show suspicious activity at Kumchang, an area about 25 miles (40 kilometers) northeast of the Yongbyon Nuclear Research Center. There 10,000 to 15,000 workers were busily creating a huge cavern beneath a mountain–the perfect site for a hidden-away nuclear facility.

It's highly likely that the space is being prepared for an underground reactor and reprocessing center where nuclear waste could be turned into bomb-grade plutonium. One *New York Times* reporter joked that U.S. officials expect the

North Koreans to claim that they are building something like "a giant underground parking garage." "There's only one problem with that explanation," the reporter noted. "The country is so poor, it has almost no cars."[1]

U.S. intelligence may have further uncovered facilities especially equipped to detonate variously sized nuclear devices. In addition, intelligence operators are monitoring at least ten underground sites also suspected of being connected to a North Korean nuclear buildup.

Such developments have severely strained the 1994 agreement with North Korea. North Korean officials have refused to allow an inspection of the large underground mountain construction site. Although they haven't gone as far as to claim that it's an underground parking lot, they continue to insist that the facility is for civilian purposes only. Meanwhile North Korea has accused the United States of trying to renege on its part of the "Agreed Framework," as Congress has been slow to authorize tens of millions of dollars in fuel shipments—the major portion of the U.S. contribution.

The North Korean government-controlled news agency openly expressed its intolerance for what it perceived as the failure of the United States to fulfill its end of the bargain, and said that its country "should no longer lend an ear to the empty promises of the United States' side, but open and readjust the frozen nuclear facilities. . . ."[2]

In response to North Korea's complaints, the U.S. State Department said that while Congress failed to immediately authorize the money for the fuel shipments, the United States fully intends to live up to its commitment. Officials stressed that although the oil shipments may have been late, the promised quota will be met. Plans for the two reactors to be installed in North Korea have also been delayed by Japan's and South Korea's failure to promptly come up with the billions of dollars they promised due to the fiscal crisis in these nations. Despite the delays, Undersecretary of State Thomas Pickering warned the North Koreans not to depart from the agreed to terms. He noted, "Anything that would happen to undermine the integrity of that agreement from the North Korean side or from the outside would be in our view, extremely lamentable and regrettable."[3]

Still, in retaliation for the lag, North Korea announced that it's temporarily halting work on dismantling its nuclear program. A high-ranking North Korean official noted that there are plans to unseal (open) the closed nuclear reactor at Yongbyon even though it was to remain permanently closed according to the Agreed Framework. Technicians have also been stopped from packing up the last of the reactor's spent fuel rods to be shipped out of North Korea. These rods contain plutonium that could be used to construct nuclear weapons.

Some nuclear weapons experts have argued that North Korea's actions, such as reopening the plant in Yongbyon, are largely symbolic since the number of rods left don't contain enough plutonium to pose a genuine nuclear threat. "This is like somebody dusting off the old .45 and making sure that it shines, but not loading it," stressed Gary Milhollin, director of the Wisconsin Project on Nuclear Arms Control. "They're sending a clever signal in our direction saying, remember, we can stop cooperating."[4]

Milhollin may well be correct in his assessment of the situation. North Korea's foreign minister Kim Yong Nam explained his country's point of view as follows, "We are

*A view of the interior of the fuel rod fabrication plant in Yongbyon, North Korea—one of several plants in the area that produce materials related to nuclear bomb production.*

keeping up our progress in implementing the nuclear freeze agreement, but the U.S. is behind. So we have now decided to slow down and suspend certain aspects of the agreement."[5] Kim further noted that when the United States has an opportunity to "catch up," North Korea fully intends to make good on all the terms of the deal.

There are other issues affecting the agreement as well. North Korea has asked the United States to drop sanctions against their country that date back to the Korean War, though their latest actions make it increasingly unlikely that this will occur. In addition North Korea has expressed disappointment in what it regards as the United States' lukewarm attempts to reduce trade barriers—a concern that had also been included in the Agreed Framework.

Testifying before Congress, Defense Secretary William J. Cohen stated that "if they [the North Koreans] can point to . . . a [serious] breach of the Agreed Framework, in a matter of weeks they can be back in the business of producing plutonium."[6] Yet there are those who believe that North Korea never planned to abide by the agreement, regardless of what the United States did. A 1998 report by the General Accounting Office, an investigative agency of Congress, indicated serious gaps in the inspection program imposed on North Korea.

According to their findings, the North Koreans may have tampered with evidence revealing that they had actually stockpiled significantly more plutonium than admitted to in the agreement. The report noted that the North Koreans will not allow the International Atomic Energy Agency to install monitoring devices on their nuclear waste tanks. This raises the question of whether the North Koreans removed some of the nuclear waste in order to camouflage prior plutonium withdrawals from the nuclear reactors.

A number of defense experts suspect that they may have even secretly built a nuclear bomb. "The danger is that the North Koreans already have nuclear weapons on the shelf," said David Albright of the Institute for Science and International Security, which studies nuclear nonproliferation issues. He added that when the 1994 U.S.-North Korea Agreed Framework was worked out "not enough thought was put into verification and that's why these kinds of problems have developed."[7]

Despite these worrisome moves on North Korea's part, in October 1998, Congress reluctantly agreed to provide the funding requested by the administration for the promised fuel oil, though it placed a number of tough conditions on the money's disbursement. These included proof that North Korea "is cooperating fully" in the canning and storage of nuclear reactor fuel rods and that North Korea is complying with all provisions of the Agreed Framework. As administration officials noted that it would be nearly impossible to meet these conditions, they indicated that the president would have to secure most of the money from other governments or invoke national security to obtain funding for the fuel oil.

Congress had also refused to release the needed fuel oil money unless the administration could certify that North Korea was not exporting ballistic missiles (which could carry nuclear warheads) to nations that support terrorists. This concern became paramount when, in late August 1998, North Korea sent a powerful new missile known as the Taepo Dong-1 over Japan and into the Pacific Ocean. The exercise demonstrated the country's aggressive missile program, making some defense experts feel apprehensive about North Korea's work on even more powerful missiles that could reach the U.S. West Coast. As Republican congressman Kurt Weldon, a member of the National Security Committee, described the feeling, "It's the first time a rogue state has launched a multistage missile. It's extremely disturbing."[8]

What especially alarms many people is that North Korea is actively engaged in the business of selling missiles, many of which can be readily outfitted with nuclear warheads. In the early 1980s, North Korean engineers were already busily reworking old Soviet scud missile designs to enhance the ranges of these rockets, making them more salable abroad.

North Korea's missile sales, which averaged about $700 million a year in the late 1980s, are its greatest source of foreign revenue. But by the 1990s the country's missile sales were down to only approximately $50 million annually, as many of North Korea's customers were now using other suppliers as well. With the country's economy at a dangerous low, North Korea is in dire need of increased currency. Some feel that sending off the powerful new missile over Japan may have been a ploy to attract more business. "What they are doing is demonstrating a new product," observed a senior administration official.[9]

Unfortunately, some of North Korea's customers hold a belligerent posture toward the United States. Korea has already shared its chemical and biological weapons expertise with Iran, Syria, and Libya and according to one White House official, "North Korea is the only unabashed seller of missile systems [that could be outfitted with nuclear warheads]. . . . " CIA director James Woolsey added, "A number of countries around the world are proliferation problems, but North Korea is in a league of its own."[10] In recent years North Korea has sold both actual missiles and the essential technology for missile systems to Syria and Iran. The United States also fears that it might soon be selling its nuclear weapons materials.

As a country strapped for both oil and cash, lately North Korean officials have resorted to selling just about anything, including drugs and counterfeit currency, along with weapons. "It's a mafia masquerading as a government," contends James Przystud of the National Defense University in Washington, D.C.[11] Another international defense analyst added, "If North Korea were not a nation, you could indict it as a continuing criminal enterprise."[12] If nuclear weapons or materials become part of its salable inventory, there's cause for serious global concern.

In the movie *The Peacemaker* actors Nicole Kidman and George Clooney are pitted against a Bosnian terrorist with a nuclear bomb tucked in his backpack. At the last minute Kidman and Clooney foil his attempts and save New York City in dashing Hollywood style. The film is pure fiction but it does leave viewers to ponder some distressing questions. Questions like:

Could terrorists ever manage to use a nuclear weapon on U.S. soil to further their aims?. . .Or could two U.S. government agents nearly single-handedly stop a terrorist scheme similar to the one depicted in the movie?

Unfortunately, the answer to the first question is yes, while a realistic response to the second is–probably not. If you disagree, just picture these scenarios:

An old freighter filled with tons of rusty scrap metal slowly makes its way toward the Potomac River. The crew seems ordinary enough and through underground black market sources they've secured all the necessary papers to enter this country. Looking at them no one would guess that they were actually terrorists on the most important mission of their lives. Yet beneath their cargo of debris, in the ship's hold, is a container with a small nuclear bomb.

The Peacemaker *is just one of a number of recent movies that deal with the threat of nuclear weapons in the hands of the wrong people. Although the specter of such large-scale destruction provides thrills, thoughtful movie watchers ponder the feasibility of the plotlines in the light of the increasing use of nuclear technology around the world.*

It was purchased from two Russian scientists desperate for cash and anxious to leave their country. Both men had worked in the Soviet defense industry for years and now found themselves unemployed and with nowhere to turn. For the price of relocating their families and themselves along with enough to start up a business, they did more than just come up with some plutonium from a dismantled Soviet warhead. They also fashioned it into a crude nuclear device that would make Washington, D.C., unrecognizable.

Or picture this. . . .

It's a beautiful spring day in our nation's capital and two young men have decided to enjoy their lunch in the park. They seem like typical college students eating their sandwiches next to what looks like a picnic cooler. They appear to be taking in the scenery when the cooler suddenly explodes. An instant later, it's over. The final death toll numbers in the thousands. The Washington Monument, the Pentagon, NASA headquarters, and many other government buildings no longer exist. The two young men with the bomb knew they were going to die, but were willing to become martyrs for what they believed in.

In recent years terrorist bombs have gone off in New York City, Oklahoma City, Tel Aviv, Paris, London, and Dublin as well as in other cities. Bruce Hoffman, an analyst for the Rand Corporation, feels that incidents like the World Trade Center bombing and the Aum Shinrikyo nerve gas attack on the Tokyo subway system are indicative of the changing face of terrorism. "The March 1995 deadly nerve gas on the Tokyo underground marks an historical watershed in terrorist tactics and weaponry," Hoffman said. "Previously, most terrorists had an aversion to the esoteric and exotic weapons of mass destruction popularized in fictional thrillers or depicted in action-hero movies and television shows. Indeed, the pattern of terrorism over three decades suggests that many groups are impelled by an inner dynamic, an organizational imperative towards escalation."[1]

So far the terrorist bombs haven't been nuclear, but that doesn't guarantee that they couldn't be in the future. The old-time terrorist cells of five to fifteen people have been replaced by groups with elaborate infrastructures that may be state sponsored or have other financial resources which would allow them to engage in broad-scale nuclear terrorism.

Aum Shinrikyo, which had been exploring the use of nuclear weapons, had over 50,000 members, more than a billion dollars in assets, and a talented staff of nuclear physicists. Yet this group escaped detection by any of the international watchdog agencies that police terrorist activities. A congressional subcommittee looking into the matter was amazed to find "that the Aum and their doomsday weapons were simply not on anybody's radar screen."[2]

Ted Taylor, formerly a chief weapons designer at the Los Alamos National Laboratories, once said. "I could build a fifteen kiloton [nuclear] bomb in my kitchen—certainly powerful enough to kill a million people in the middle of Manhattan."[3] Taylor added that a terrorist group could construct a nuclear bomb small enough to be easily transported—the finished product would fit into the trunk of a Volkswagen Beetle with room to spare.

However, there are drawbacks to using plutonium to make a nuclear bomb, and a terrorist sophisticated enough to construct one would probably know this. For one thing, plutonium can be readily detected in transit by special instruments. The plutonium would also contain other plutonium isotopes that make it hard to work with.

But before you breathe a sigh of relief, consider this. Senator Richard Lugar of Indiana pointed out that there's a very real danger of terrorists going "nuclear" using highly enriched uranium. While plutonium has to be made in a nuclear reactor, uranium occurs naturally in the environment. Although it is too diluted in these forms for terrorist use, it's likely that enough highly enriched uranium can be purchased on the international black market to create a bomb.

The simplest type of bomb to make with highly enriched uranium would be a "gun-barrel" type of device. Physicist Luis Alvarez described the ease of this approach, pointing out, "With modern weapons-grade uranium . . . terrorists, if they had such material, would have a good chance of setting off a high yield explosion simply by dropping one half of the material onto the other half. Most people seem unaware that if separated [highly enriched] uranium is at hand, it's a trivial job to set off a nuclear explosion. . . . Even a high school kid could make a bomb in short order."[4]

There are other reasons why enriched uranium would hold appeal for terrorists. The low radioactivity of a uranium bomb permits it to be handled without protective gloves as well as makes it more difficult to be picked up by detection devices. It's also easier than plutonium to purchase worldwide.

Although nuclear materials may be more available than in the past, terrorists desiring a nuclear bomb wouldn't necessarily have to build one. There's also the possibility of purchasing a nuclear device on the black market or stealing a bomb. In addition, authorities are concerned that terrorists might even lace a conventional bomb with radioactive material. Spread throughout an area by the explosion, the results would be detrimental to both the population and land. "You really don't need to have a mushroom cloud to have an effective nuclear device," noted Peter S. Probst, who contributed to a Pentagon study on terrorism.[5]

The increased terrorist nuclear threat has called for a stepped-up U.S. response on various levels. In 1995, Congress passed the Comprehensive Antiterrorism Act, which provides stiffer criminal penalties for any American citizen who illegally obtains nuclear materials. And in May 1998, President Clinton appointed a national coordinator for security, infrastructure protection, and counterterrorism to "bring the full force of our resources to bear swiftly and effectively."[6] The efforts of U.S. intelligence agencies in this area have been enhanced as well.

The Nuclear Emergency Search Team (NEST), a little known counterterrorism task force of about one thousand people, has been readied as well. NEST members include physicists, engineers, technicians, and others from various nuclear laboratories, arsenals, and Energy Department offices. If there's a nuclear bomb threat or a tip that a nuclear bomb is set to explode, NEST would be called to locate the device, identify its strength, and disable it.

NEST operators are trained to perform a number of different tasks depending on their skills. NEST scientists at a weapons laboratory complex construct homemade bombs out of parts found in hardware stores and Radio Shack us-

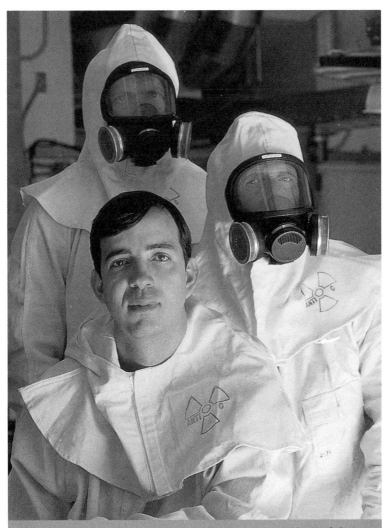

No, this is not another movie clip. These are members of the nuclear bomb dismantling team, some of the more than one thousand employees of NEST. Since its founding in 1975, the group has evaluated more than 110 nuclear threats, and has actually mobilized to deal with 30 of them—all of which were hoaxes.

ing a nuclear fuel that is readily obtainable internationally on the black market. The idea behind this exercise is to learn the various ways these devices can be put together so that in an emergency they could be quickly and safely dismantled. Of course, that doesn't mean that a suspected nuclear bomb would always be taken apart by a person on the team. In some cases a wheeled robot known as an Automated Tether-Operated Manipulator (ATOM) may be called in to do the job. The robot has a remote control arm that can be controlled from a distance.

But before you can disengage a bomb, you have to find it. The Department of Energy's aerial-surveillance aircraft would help to narrow the search zone by identifying radiation hot spots, while a NEST computer containing key pages from spy novels determined whether a written threat was genuine or if the culprit merely lifted a few paragraphs from a popular book.

Much of the actual bomb search conducted by NEST would be done in minivans outfitted with detection devices capable of pinpointing a nuclear bomb. Search team members would also work on foot, carrying radiation detectors small enough to fit into a briefcase or backpack. NEST participants practice their craft in regularly conducted training sessions. Mirage Gold was the code name for one such endeavor held in New Orleans in October 1994. After combing the city, NEST team members found the package they were looking for hidden on a naval base not far from the city.

Presently NEST does not operate out of the country, but some feel it might be called upon to do so in the future. Nuclear scientist John Nuckolls of Livermore Lab (a nuclear weapons development site) believes that some day this U.S. preparedness force will join others in an international team. "The destruction of any city in the world by nuclear terrorists would threaten all cities and all nations," he insists.[7] If he's right, everyone's at risk, and nuclear counterterrorism measures are a vital priority.

In a rapidly changing nuclear world, there's been an ongoing debate about the role the United States should take. Some feel that the nation should concentrate on bolstering its defenses against a possible nuclear attack from a terrorist group or "outlaw" nation. Others believe that while this is important, more attention should be focused on nuclear disarmament efforts. They insist that the fewer nuclear weapons in the world, the less chance for an attack or accident.

Recently a great deal of emphasis has been placed on developing and deploying a national missile system in which a defensive missile can track and destroy an incoming missile. The system is based on a "hit to kill" principle. A missile is sent up to hit and kill the incoming missile before it reaches its target.

In 1983, President Ronald Reagan initiated work on an elaborate futuristic space-based missile defense system that would ideally create an impenetrable shield against the awesome threat of a massive Soviet missile attack. Dubbed

Star Wars, it was a vision that never became a reality. After sixteen years of research and $60 billion, the Star Wars scientists still couldn't produce a system that worked.

Early in his presidency, Bill Clinton had not heartily supported funding for continuing Star Wars research. Starting out in the White House, Clinton's foreign policy centered more on arms-control advocacy than a continuing dependence on advanced weaponry. Even as late as 1998, President Clinton returned to Los Alamos, the laboratory where the first atom bomb was created, to once again call for an end to the nuclear arms race.

"Los Alamos in so many ways is the place that forever changed the twentieth century," Clinton told his audience there. "For more than fifty years since we first split the atom and unleashed its awesome force, the nuclear threat has hovered over our heads. Throughout the Cold War and the arms race, it has been an ever-present threat to our people and the people of the world. . . . Today there is not a single Russian missile pointed at America's children. But we have to do more."[1]

Clinton had sent the Comprehensive Test-Ban Treaty to the Senate for ratification after it was signed by the United States and 154 other nations. The United States had been the first country to sign the treaty in 1996, but it had to be ratified by all the nuclear-capable nations to go into effect. President Clinton, however, was dealt a humiliating defeat when the Senate rejected the landmark treaty in October 1999, making it the first time in U.S. history that the Senate rejected an arms control agreement.

Those in favor of the treaty had stressed that the United States' present nuclear weapons are far ahead of those of other countries and that the treaty would freeze the lesser technology of other nuclear powers way behind those of the United States. In support of the treaty, Clinton said that a high-tech program for monitoring nuclear weapons would make actual testing unnecessary. John Browne, director of the Los Alamos facility, affirmed that scientists could check older weapons for cracks and other possible problems by simulating nuclear explosions on supercomputers in the lab. Treaty proponents further maintained that rejection of the treaty would make the world an increasingly danger-ous place, as newly emerging nuclear powers, like India and Pakistan, might feel they had to continue testing to keep up with stronger nations.

Nevertheless, opponents of the treaty saw the pact as a Cold War relic that failed to address genuine nuclear concerns in today's world. They said it would have little impact on nations secretly doing nuclear research or states like Iraq and North Korea that have been known to sign treaties and then lie about their country's nuclear plans and activities. Treaty critics also argued that the treaty of-fered scant protection against terrorists who either steal or buy "loose nukes" from countries in need of quick cash or are supported by "outlaw" states.

Despite the Senate's rejection of the treaty, Secretary of State Madeleine Albright insists that the United States is not planning to conduct nuclear tests and continues to discourage other nations from doing so. In addition, treaty supporters have taken steps to insure that the Senate's rejection didn't permanently kill the treaty. They secured

Although the political nuclear disarmament process is painfully slow, there is progress. The top picture shows American plant workers in Amarillo, Texas, disassembling a retired nuclear weapon—while the bottom one shows a Russian worker turning retired missiles into refrigerators and vacuum cleaners.

a parliamentary ruling that would permit it to be brought before the Senate again in the future. President Clinton has vowed that the fight for the treaty is not over and has urged other nations to ratify it in the hope that the United States will eventually join them.

Yet even prior to the Senate's rejection of the pact, the United States had begun to shift its thinking and policy to deal with areas of concern not addressed by the treaty. One pivotal point occurred in July 1998, when a special government commission headed by former Defense Secretary Donald Rumsfeld turned in an unsettling report. The commission announced that Iran, Iraq, or North Korea would be capable of launching a nuclear missile at the United States within five years. The commission was not alone in its findings. Lester Lyles, director of the Ballistic Missile Defense Organization, further predicted in 1998 that North Korea's Taepo Dong-1 missile first fired across Japan could threaten the United States within "a couple of years."[2]

At that point President Clinton began to seriously consider the merits of a national missile defense system, although he prefers a smaller, scaled-down version of Star Wars. This system would largely consist of space-based detection stations to spot and track an incoming missile and ground-based missiles to destroy the attack missile. The proposed revamped system would not be a suitable defense against a massive nuclear attack from a nation with a substantial nuclear arsenal but would protect all fifty states from a small nuclear attack from a nation such as Iraq, Iran, or North Korea. The president proposed spending $6.6 billion in his defense budget for the system, which would be built over a six-year period and deployed by 2005.

While Clinton wants the funds allotted for the program, he'll decide if and when the system will be built at a later date, once the developmental work has shown that the mini-Star Wars defense is effective.

Not everyone agrees with President Clinton's nuclear defense choices. Critics argue that Clinton's national missile defense will fail as surely as Ronald Reagan's Star Wars did, since shooting down high-speed missiles is only easy in the movies. They stress that despite all the Reagan-era money spent on a national missile defense system, not a single usable weapon has been produced—adding that out of fifteen test flights only two hit the incoming target. When Clinton proposed a national missile defense in his military spending budget, there hadn't been a single successful test since 1992.

Yet those in favor of a streamlined missile defense system claim that over the years there have been numerous valuable breakthroughs in both network-computing and sensor technology. They've further insisted that the new system would be substantially less complicated and therefore easier to design and build than the one proposed by President Reagan. Lieutenant Colonel Richard A. Lehner, a spokesperson for the national missile defense program at the Pentagon, summed up the sentiment saying, "Those of us who work in the program are very confident we're going to have a working system and we're going to have it soon."[3]

In further discussing the system, the chairman of the Joint Chiefs of Staff, General Henry H. Shelton, testified before the Armed Services Committee that although the Pentagon had sufficient resources to continue developing the national missile defense system, the administration was "also putting money into the program so that at the time that we have the technology, if in fact the threat justifies it, then we could go ahead with the fielding."[4]

But even if the Defense Department now manages to create a well-functioning national missile system, would it really protect the entire nation? Many people don't believe that a nuclear attack on the United States is going to come through missiles outfitted with nuclear warheads. Instead they feel that an "outlaw" state or a group of independent terrorists would be more likely to bring a nuclear bomb to a major U.S. city in a suitcase, a rental truck, or by freighter.

According to Republican senator John Kyl, who serves on the Senate Select Committee on Intelligence and is chairman of the Judiciary Subcommittee on Technology, Terrorism, and Government Information, "Even a rogue state is very unlikely to threaten the United States by building an ICBM [intercontinental ballistic missile]. Rather any state or group that decided on the risky course of seeking to coerce the United States government by threatening nuclear destruction would seek to smuggle a nuclear device into the United States or demonstrate a capacity to explode one offshore; an ABM [antiballistic missile] defense thus would not be an effective defense."[5]

Secretary of Defense William Cohen even admitted that the Joint Chiefs of Staff tend to "worry more about a suitcase bomb going off in one of our cities." "Very few countries are going to launch an ICBM," Cohen explained, "knowing that they are going to face virtual elimination [as a result of U.S. retaliation]."[6]

Building a national missile defense system also presents diplomatic difficulties. The Chinese are staunchly opposed to the United States deploying antimissile defenses around the American mainland. In a January 1999 speech in Washington, D.C., China's senior arms control officer Sha Zukang insinuated that if the United States were to build its proposed national missile defense system, China would feel pressed to enhance its intercontinental nuclear ability as well. "If a country, in addition to its offensive power, seeks to develop advanced theater missiles or even national missile defense," Sha said, "then other countries will be forced to develop more advanced offensive missiles." He added, "This will give rise to a new arms race."[7]

Russia is also against the proposed system as it violates the 1972 Anti-Ballistic Missile Treaty, which limits the amount, type, and placement of U.S. and Soviet missile defenses. While the treaty has been referred to as "a cornerstone of strategic stability," proponents of the national missile defense system stress that treaties can be renegotiated.

The Russians, however, are adamantly against the system and are not predisposed to revamping the treaty. They've further implied that in violating the 1972 treaty, the United States jeopardizes the chances for further Russian nuclear arms reduction. As Russian foreign minister Igor Ivanov told Secretary of State Madeleine Albright and Secretary of Defense William Cohen, "We believe that further cuts in strategic offensive weapons can be done only if there is a clear vision for preserving and observing the ABM treaty."[8]

In response, Ms. Albright has tried to work with the Russians stressing that the United States has to act responsibly in dealing with a growing concern posed by "outlaw" nations and state supported terrorists. "We have to deal with the threats of the day, not of the previous day or tomorrow," she explained.[9]

The Anti-Ballistic Missile Treaty permits either side to back out with six months notice "if it decides that extraordinary events related to the subject matter of the treaty have jeopardized its supreme interests."[10] Defense Secretary William Cohen sees that as a possibility in light of the growing threat to U.S. security. "We will need to renegotiate changes to the ABM treaty," Cohen said. "If the Russians don't agree, we have the option to opt out of the treaty."[11] Yet abandoning the treaty would probably not be in the United States' best interests since it might be seen as indicating a lack of commitment to other treaties.

Critics of the national missile defense system continue to insist that the billions spent on it would be more wisely used on some high-gear diplomacy. They'd like to see the money go into efforts to stop terrorists and hostile nations from acquiring nuclear weapons as well as to further arms reductions with Russia. As Michael Klare, author of *Rogue States and Nuclear Outlaws*, noted, ". . . the answer . . . is through arms control. For one-one-thousandth of the expense of Star Wars, we would be accelerating the decommissioning of Russian missiles and buying up the missiles of Iran, Iraq, and North Korea."[12]

Is he right or do advanced weapons proponents have a better solution? Opinions differ and it may be too soon to know the answer. Meanwhile policies and practices continue to be reassessed as we struggle to find a balance in the new nuclear reality.

## SOURCE NOTES

**Chapter 1**
1. David Hughes, "When Terrorists Go Nuclear: The Ingredients and Information Have Never Been More Available," *Popular Mechanics*, January 1996, p. 56.

**Chapter 2**
1. "Krasnoyarsk-26-Secret City." 60 Minutes CBS News, (transcript) vol. XXXII no. 17, 1/13/99.
2. Matthew Bunn, "Pre-empting A Russian Nuclear Meltdown," *Knight-Ridder/Tribune News Service*, December 24, 1998, p. 3.
3. Joseph Cirincione, "Nuclear Free-Fall," *The Washington Quarterly*, Winter 1999, p. 20.
4. Cirincione, "Nuclear Free-Fall."
5. "Krasnoyarsk-26–Secret City."
6. Cirincione, "Nuclear Free-Fall."
7. Cirincione, "Nuclear Free-Fall."
8. Center for Defense Information, "U.S.-Russian Relations: Avoiding a New Cold War," *America's Defense Monitor*, 1998, vol. XXVII, Issue 5, p. 1.
9. Center for Defense Information, "U.S.-Russian Relations."
10. Cirincione, "Nuclear Free-Fall."

11. Kurt Weldon, "An Urgent Need For A Strong Missile Defense," *USA Today*, May 1997, p. 2.
12. "Krasnoyarsk-26-Secret City."
13. "Krasnoyarsk-26-Secret City."
14. "Krasnoyarsk-26-Secret City."
15. Robert S. Boyd, "Russian Nuclear Materials Remain Unprotected From Terrorists," *Knight-Ridder/Tribune News Service*, April 17, 1997, p. 2.
16. Boyd, "Russian Nuclear Materials."
17. Boyd, "Russian Nuclear Materials."
18. Amanda Bichsel, "How the GOP Learned to Love the Bomb," *Washington Monthly*, November 1995, p. 26.
19. Malcolm Gray and William Lowther, "The Loose Nukes," *Maclean's*, April 22, 1996, p. 24.
20. Center For Defense Information, "Avoiding a New Cold War," *The Defense Monitor*, vol. XXVII, issue 5, 1998, p. 1.
21. Amanda Bichsel, "How the GOP Learned to Love the Bomb."
22. Steven Lee Myers, "U.S. Urged to Reduce Nuclear Arsenal to Revive Russian Talks," *The New York Times*, February 26, 1999, p. A8.
23. Myers, "U.S. Urged to Reduce Nuclear Arsenal."

## Chapter 3
1. Center for Defense Information, "Nuclear Power, Nuclear Weapons," *America's Defense Monitor*, Program No. 1023, Initial Broadcast, February 16, 1997.
2. Richard Butler, "Why UNSCOM Matters," *Newsweek*, November 23, 1998, p. 32.
3. Barbara Slavin, "Iraqi Weapons Inspectors Increasingly Ineffective," *USA Today*, November 3, 1998, p. 1A.
4. Slavin, "Iraqi Weapons Inspectors."
5. Romesh Ratnesar, "What Good Did It Do?", *Time*, December 26, 1998, p. 70.
6. Michael Kilran, "Pentagon Says Strike Weakened Iraq's Military," *Knight-Ridder/Tribune News Service*, December 2, 1998, p. 1.

7. Richard Parker, "Controlling Saddam Hussein Will Be a Long-Term Challenge," *Knight-Ridder/Tribune News Service*, December 21, 1998, p. 3.
8. Ratnesar, "What Good Did It Do?"
9. Ratnesar, "What Good Did It Do?"
10. Parker, "Controlling Saddam Hussein."
11. Parker, "Controlling Saddam Hussein."
12. Parker, "Controlling Saddam Hussein."
13. Butler, "Why UNSCOM Matters."
14. "Saddam's Bombmaker," 60 Minutes II CBS, January 27, 1999.
15. "Saddam's Bombmaker."
16. "Saddam's Bombmaker."
17. "Saddam's Bombmaker."
18. Barbara Crossette. "Iraq Has a Network of Outside Help on Arms, Experts Say," *The New York Times*, November 20, 1998, p. A3.
19. Crossette, "Iraq Has a Network."
20. Crossette, "Iraq Has a Network."
21. Crossette, "Iraq Has a Network."
22. Parker, "Controlling Saddam Hussein."
23. Peter Tarnoff, "Containing Iran," *U.S. Department of State Dispatch*, November 13, 1995, p. 32.
24. Kenneth R. Timmerman, "Missile Threat From Iran," *Reader's Digest* (Large Print Edition), January 1998, p. 82.
25. Timmerman, "Missile Threat From Iran."
26. "U.S. Offers Missile Data to Gulf Allies," *The Miami Herald*, March 9, 1999, p. 9A.
27. Rodney W. Jones and Mark G. McDonough, *Tracking Nuclear Proliferation: A Guide in Maps and Charts* (Washington, D.C.: Carnegie Endowment For International Peace, 1998), p. 215.
28. Jones and McDonough, *Tracking Nuclear Proliferation.*

**Chapter 4**

1. Carol Leonning, "Helms Says India's Detonation Proves He's Right About a Nuclear Treaty," *Knight-Ridder/Tribune*

*News Service,* May 13, 1998, p. 1.

2. Russell Watson, "Explosion of Self-Esteem," *Newsweek,* May 25, 1998, p. 32B.
3. Center for Defense Information, "Nuclear War Between India and Pakistan?" *America's Defense Monitor,* 1998, p. 4.
4. Center for Defense Information, "Nuclear War Between India and Pakistan?"
5. Watson, "Explosion of Self-Esteem."
6. Watson, "Explosion of Self-Esteem."
7. Michael Hirsh and John Barry, "Nuclear Jitters," *Newsweek,* June 8, 1998, p. 22.
8. Hirsh and Barry, "Nuclear Jitters."
9. Watson, "Explosion of Self-Esteem."
10. Marc Kaufman, "Pakistan Had No Choice But to Answer India's Nuclear Tests With Their Own Test," *Knight-Ridder/ Tribune News Service,* May 28, 1998, p. 2.
11. Kaufman, "Pakistan Had No Choice."
12. Hirsh and Barry, "Nuclear Jitters."
13. Hirsh and Barry, "Nuclear Jitters."
14. Kaufman, "Pakistan Had No Choice."
15. Andrew Koch, "Subcontinental Missiles," *Bulletin of Atomic Scientists,* July/August 1998, p. 49.
16. Koch, "Subcontinental Missiles."
17. Steven Thomma, "U.S. Officials Are Skeptical About Impact of Sanctions on India and Pakistan," *Knight-Ridder/ Tribune News Service,* May 28, 1998, p. 2.
18. Douglas Walker, "China's Arms Race," *Time,* February 1, 1999, p. 31.
19. David E. Sanger, "U.S. Says It Caught a Chinese Smuggler Seeking Gyroscopes That Can Guide Missiles," *The New York Times,* March 1, 1999, p. A8.
20. Brian Duffy and Warren P. Strobel, "When Rocket Science Turns Troublesome," *U.S. News & World Report,* December 21, 1998, p. 32.
21. Warren P. Strobel, "America's Stolen Thunder," *U.S. News & World Report,* June 7, 1999, p. 38.
22. Walker, "China's Arms Race."

23. Duffy and Strobel, "When Rocket Science Turns Trouble-some."
24. Thomma, "U.S. Officials Are Skeptical."
25. Thomma, "U.S. Officials Are Skeptical."
26. Hirsh and Barry, "Nuclear Jitters."
27. Celia W. Dugger, "India's Testing Issue," *The New York Times*, December 5, 1998, p. A8.
28. Barry Bearah, "India, Pakistan Agree To Curb Nuclear Risk, Negotiate on Kashmir and Other Issues," *The Miami Herald*, February 22, 1999, p. 7A.
29. Bearah, "India, Pakistan Agree."
30. Bearah, "India, Pakistan Agree."
31. Thomma, "U.S. Officials Are Skeptical."

## Chapter 5

1. David E. Sanger, "Underground Test Site May Hide North Korean Nuclear Reactor," *The New York Times*, August 23, 1998, p. 2.
2. Elisabeth Rosenthal, "North Korea Says It Will Unseal Reactor," *The New York Times*, May 13, 1998, p. 10A.
3. Rosenthal, "North Korea Says It Will Unseal Reactor."
4. Rosenthal, "North Korea Says It Will Unseal Reactor."
5. Philip Shenon, "North Korean Nuclear Arms Pact Reported Near Breakdown," *The New York Times*, December 6, 1998, p. 16.
6. Shenon, "North Korean Nuclear Arms Pact."
7. Philip Shenon, "North Korea Said to Block Inspection of Nuclear Sites," *The New York Times*, July 15, 1998, p. 10.
8. Donald MacIntyre, "Missile With a Message," *Time*, September 14, 1998, p. 55.
9. Tim Zimmerman, "Arms Merchant to the World," *U.S. News & World Report*, April 4, 1994, p. 37.
10. Zimmerman, "Arms Merchant to the World."
11. David E. Kaplan, "The Wiseguy Regime," *U.S. News & World Report*, February 15, 1999, p. 36.
12. Kaplan, "The Wiseguy Regime."

## Chapter 6

1. John Leifer, "Apocalypse Ahead: Everyone's Talking About the Film 'The Peacemaker'—But When It Comes To Nuclear Terrorism, The Truth Is Scarier Than Fiction," *Washington Monthly*, November 1997, p. 30.
2. Leifer, "Apocalypse Ahead."
3. Leifer, "Apocalypse Ahead."
4. Leifer, "Apocalypse Ahead."
5. David Hughes, "When Terrorists Go Nuclear: The Ingredients and Information Have Never Been More Available," *Popular Mechanics*, January 1996, p. 56.
6. Ashton Carter, John M. Deutch, and Philip Zelikow, "Catastrophic Terrorism," *Foreign Affairs*, November 1998, p. 80.
7. Douglas Waller, "Nuclear Ninjas: A New Kind of SWAT Team Hunts Atomic Terrorists," *Time*, January 8, 1996, p. 39.

## Chapter 7

1. Jodi Enda, "Clinton Calls for an End to Nuclear Arms," *Knight-Ridder/Tribune News Service*, February 3, 1998, p. 2.
2. "A Sensible Missile Defense," *USA Today*, January 27, 1999, p. 3.
3. Steven Lee Myers, "Clinton to Pledge $7 Billion for Missile Defense System," *The New York Times*, January 7, 1999, p. A28.
4. Myers, "Clinton To Pledge $7 Billion."
5. Jon Kyl and Morton Halperin, "Is the White House's Nuclear Arms Policy on the Wrong Track," *Insight on the News*, November 17, 1997, p. 24.
6. Mark Thompson, "Star Wars: The Sequel," *Time*, February 22, 1999, p. 51.
7. David E. Sanger and Erik Echolm, "Will Beijing's Nuclear Arsenal Stay Small Or Will It Mushroom," *The New York Times*, March 15, 1999, p. 1.
8. Thompson, "Star Wars: The Sequel."

9. Jane Perlez, "Albright Seeks to Reassure Moscow on Star Wars Plan," *The New York Times*, January 25, 1999, p. A6.

10. Steven Lee Myers, "U.S. Asking Russia to Ease the Pact on Missile Defense," *The New York Times*, January 21, 1999, p. 17.

11. Michael Barone, "Stopping Nuclear Blackmail," *U.S. News & World Report*, March 8, 1999, p. 31.

12. "Star Wars Forever," *The Progressive*, September 1998, p. 9.

## Books

Bundy, McGeorge. *Reducing Nuclear Danger: The Road Away From the Brink*. New York: Council on Foreign Relations Press, 1993.

Cheney, Glenn Alan. *They Never Knew: The Victims of Nuclear Testing*. Danbury, CT: Franklin Watts, 1996.

Euron, Yair. *Israel's Nuclear Dilemma*. Ithaca, NY: Cornell University Press, 1994.

Gold, Susan Dudley. *Arms Control*. Brookfield, CT: Twenty-First Century Books, 1997.

Murphy, Wendy B. *Nuclear Medicine*. New York: Chelsea House Publishers, 1994.

Office of Technology Assessment. *Proliferation of Weapons of Mass Destruction: Assessing the Risks*. Washington, DC: U.S. Congress, 1993.

Pry, Peter Vincent. *War Scare: Nuclear Countdown After the Soviet Fall*. Atlanta, GA: Turner Publications, 1997.

Sagan, Scott Douglass. *The Spread Of Nuclear Weapons: A Debate*. New York: W. W. Norton, 1995.

Turner, Stansfield. *Caging the Nuclear Genie: An American Challenge for Global Security.* Boulder, CO: Westview Press, 1997.

U.S. Arms Control and Disarmament Agency. *Comprehensive Nuclear Test-Ban Treaty.* Washington, DC: U.S. Government Printing Office, 1998.

Yamazaki, James N. *Children of the Atomic Bomb: An American Physician's Memoir Of Nagasaki, Hiroshima, and the Marshall Islands.* Durham, NC: Duke University Press, 1995.


**Articles**

Eckholm, Eric. "China Calls Assertion That It Stole U.S. Nuclear Arms Designs Unfounded." *The New York Times,* March 8, 1999, p. A8.

"Firefighters Get Help In Fighting Terrorism." *The New York Times,* March 15, 1999, p. A13.

Fox, Thomas C. "Getting Beyond The Deterrent Paradox." *National Catholic Reporter,* March 21, 1997, p. 28.

Goodwin, Irwin. "At Last, Nuclear Powers Sign Comprehensive Test Ban But Doubts Remain on Nonsigners and Subcritical Tests." *Physics Today,* December 1996, p. 37.

Greenberger, Robert S. "Pakistan's Premier Says He Would Sign Nuclear Treaty, Under Some Conditions." *The Wall Street Journal,* September 24, 1998, p. A4.

"Japan: Money For North Korea." *The New York Times,* October 23, 1998, p. A8.

Landay, Jonathan S., "A Decade Of Nuclear Cuts Stall." *The Christian Science Monitor,* June 22, 1998, p. 1.

Mann, Paul. "Deficit Pressures Hobble Anti-Proliferation Efforts." *Aviation Week & Space Technology,* June 17, 1996, p. 64.

"North Korea: Aid For Two Reactors." *The New York Times*, November 11, 1998, p. A8.

Risen, James, and Jeff Gerth, "China Stole Nuclear Secrets for Bombs, U.S. Aides Say." *The New York Times*, March 8, 1999, p. 1.

Weisman, Jonathan. "Nuclear Test-Ban Up Next." *Congressional Quarterly Weekly Report*, September 14, 1996, p. 2608.

Children's Campaign
for Nuclear Disarmament (CCND)
14 Everit St.
New Haven, CT 06511


Council for a Livable World (CLW)
110 Maryland Ave. NE, Ste. 409
Washington, D.C. 20002
http://www.clw.org/pub/clw/

Council for a Livable World
Education Fund (CLWEF)
110 Maryland Ave NE, Ste. 201
Washington, D.C. 20002
http://www.clw.org

Disarm Education Fund (DEF)
36 E. 12th St., 6th Fl.
NewYork, NY 10003
http://www.disarm.org

Global Issues Resource Center (GIRC)
Eastern Campus–East 1
420 Richmond Rd.

Cleveland, OH 44122
http://www.tri-cccon.us/east/docs/gir/default.htm

Grandmothers for Peace International (GPI)
9444 Medstead Way
Elk Grove, CA 95758
http://www.grandmothersforpeace.org

Institute for Defense and Disarmament Studies (IDDS)
675 Massachusetts Ave., 8th Fl.
Cambridge, MA 02139
http://www.idds.org

International Physicians for the Prevention of Nuclear War
(IPPNW)
126 Rogers St.
Cambridge, MA 02142
http://www.healthnet.org/ippnw

Lawyers Alliance for World Security (LAWS)
1901 Pennsylvania Ave. NW, Ste. 802
Washington, D.C. 20077
http://www.lawscms.org

Lawyers' Committee on
Nuclear Policy (LCNP)
666 Broadway, Ste. 625
New York, NY 10012
http://www.ddh.nl/org/ialana/index.html

Nuclear Control Institute (NCI)
1000 Connecticut Ave. NW, Ste. 804
Washington, D.C. 20036
http://www.nci.org/

Nuclear Information and Resource Service (NIRS)
1424 16th St. NW, No. 404
Washington, D.C. 20036
http://www.nirs.org

Nukewatch
PO Box 649
Luck, WI 54853-0649
http://www.serve.gvaughn/nukewatch/index/html

Peace Action
1819 H St. NW, Ste. 420
Washington, D.C. 20006-3603
http://www.webcom.com/peaceact/

Peace Action Education Fund
(PAEF)
1819 H St. NW, Ste. 425
Washington, D.C. 20006-3603
http://www.webcom.com/peaceact/

Peace Pac (PP)
110 Maryland Ave. NE, Ste. 409
Washington, D.C. 20002
http://www.ciw.org

Physicians for Social Responsibility (PSR)
1101 14th St., 7th Fl.
Washington, D.C. 20005
http://www.psr.org

Progressive Foundation (PF)
PO Box 649
Luck, WI 54853-0649
http:///www.serve.gvaughn/nukewatch/index/html

World Peacemakers (WP)
11427 Scottsbury Ter.
Germantown, MD 20876
http://www.nonviolence.org/worldpeacemakers/

INDEX

125